BARRON'S
WHIZ
QUIZ
SERIES

WHO WHAT WHEN WHERE WHY

In the World of

POLITICS

by
Carol Haas
Attorney and Newspaper Columnist

with cartoon illustrations by

S0-BAY-893

BARRON'S
New York • London • Toronto • Sydney

All inquiries should be addressed to:
Barron's Educational Series, Inc.
250 Wireless Boulevard
Hauppauge, New York 11788

Library of Congress Catalog Card No. 90-29871

International Standard Book No. 0-8120-4520-3

Library of Congress Cataloging in Publication Data
Haas, Carol.
    Who, what, when, where, why—in the world of politics /
  by Carol Haas : with cartoon illustrations by Tom Kerr.
        p.   cm. — (Barron's whiz quiz series)
      ISBN 0-8120-4520-3
      1. United States—Politics and government—
Miscellanea.
    I. Title.   II. Series.
    JK34.H22   1991
    320.973—dc20   90-29871
                                                         CIP

PRINTED IN THE UNITED STATES OF AMERICA
1 2 3 4   5500   9 8 7 6 5 4 3 2 1

To Ken, Adam, and Jake

Contents

	Introduction	ix
1	America's Chief Executives	1
2	The Lawmakers on Capitol Hill	29
3	The U.S. Supreme Court	51
4	The Campaign Trail	75
5	Political Parties and Organizations	101
6	Events and Issues	125
7	The Media	151
8	Scandals	177
9	Famous and Infamous Words	209
10	International Politics	229

Introduction

Politicians take their profession pretty seriously—and rightfully so. After all, the things they believe in, work for, and eventually act upon, shape all of our lives, sometimes for the good, sometimes not.

But the truth is, politics and the people involved with it are often rather funny. Humorist Will Rogers once said, "I don't make jokes, I just watch the government and report the facts."

So here's a fun book on politics—the "who, what, when, where, and why" about the political process.

This isn't meant to be an all inclusive look at politics—it's impossible to fit over 200 years into 200-plus pages! But hopefully we'll be touching on the more important and entertaining facts about the political process and its colorful cast of characters.

Most of this book is about American politics.

But we'd be ignoring some of the most interesting politicians and important events if we disregarded the rest of the world, so we've included a chapter on international politics as well.

Reduced to basics, politics is the struggle for power. We'll be looking at the people who have vied for that power and have used it to shape governments: the presidents, prime ministers, governors, mayors, senators, congressmen, Supreme Court justices, and ordinary people who believed in and fought for a political cause. We'll be testing you on some of the things they've said—some memorable, some shocking, some prophetic, some brutally honest, and some that were just out-and-out lies!

Our system of government depends on a delicate balance of power, particularly among the three branches of government, designed to ensure that no one branch—the executive, legislative, or judicial—wields more power than the others. We'll be quizzing you on all three branches, each with its own chapter.

We certainly couldn't ignore the elective process, a politician's method of gaining power in political office. So we've included a chapter about elections—from the campaign, to the convention, through the actual election, and finally the inauguration—as well as a chapter about political parties and organizations.

Civil rights, the military draft, feminism, and freedom of speech are just a few of the issues that have influenced American politics throughout our history, resulting in protests, sometimes bloodshed, and often new legislation or court decisions. We'll be testing you on some of the more important events and issues, as well as on those who report them—the news media, that group of nonpartisans with the power to create or destroy political careers.

Unfortunately, politicians are mere mortals and some have been known to succumb to the temptations offered by power and money, so we've included an entire chapter on those politicians who became involved in scandals.

Within each chapter, you'll find a mixture of open-ended, multiple-choice, and matching questions. They vary in difficulty; some may come quite easily, others could require digging into your memory bank, while still others may completely stump you. But, whether you find them simple or difficult, you'll find them fun, and you'll gain a better understanding of our political process and heritage.

This book is the result of the work of many people. I'd like to express special thanks to Grace Freedson, Judy Makover, and Diane Roth at Barron's Educational Series for all their work and encouragement, as well as Professor Robert Geise who checked each and every fact for accuracy.

Personal thanks to my husband Ken and two boys, Adam and Jake, for all their support.

Now it's time to sit back and find out what you know about politics. I think Senator Eugene McCarthy had an interesting perspective on the whole subject: "Being in politics is like being a football coach. You have to be smart enough to understand the game, and dumb enough to think it's important." Let's see whether you understand the game.

America's Chief
Executives

Thomas Jefferson defined the presidency as "splendid misery." Harry Truman called it a "prison." Nevertheless, there is something about that exalted position that makes sane men and women willing to give up comfortable lives and lucrative professions to serve as the Chief Executive. How much do you know about those individuals, their second-in-command, and the rest of the executive branch?

❶ Who was the only president to serve two nonconsecutive terms?

❷ Which president was impeached but avoided conviction by only one vote?

3 When Richard Nixon refused to appear before a congressional committee investigating Watergate, what privilege did he invoke?

4 Which president was in office when the Equal Rights Amendment failed ratification, when 12,000 U.S. air traffic controllers went on strike, and when the Social Security system received a shot in the arm?

5 Baseball phenom Babe Ruth sued the Curtiss Candy Company when it unveiled the "Baby Ruth" candy bar because he was sure that the company was unfairly enriching itself by exploiting his name. Curtiss successfully responded to the suit, saying that Babe Ruth was not the namesake of the bar. Who was the candy bar named after?

6 When Franklin Delano Roosevelt served as New York's governor and then as president of the United States, he surrounded himself with a group of advisors. What was the group called?

7 In the line of presidential succession, the vice president takes over in the case of death, resignation, or removal from office of the president. Who is next in line?

8 President Dwight Eisenhower renamed the presidential retreat Camp David. What was its name prior to the change?

9 New York City's flamboyant mayor from 1971 to 1989 is credited with engineering the city's financial bailout in the late 1970s. Name him.

10 Which president was once the governor of the Philippines?

11 Name the governor of Pennsylvania who in 1924 convicted and sentenced a male, black Labrador retriever to life imprisonment.

12 Incoming presidents sometimes feel the need to convince their constituents that things will be better with them at the helm, often calling their policies "new." Match the following Democratic presidents with their program:

President	Program
1. John F. Kennedy	**(a)** The New Federalism
2. Theodore Roosevelt	**(b)** The New Freedom
3. Franklin D. Roosevelt	**(c)** The New Frontier
4. Woodrow Wilson	**(d)** The New Deal
5. Richard Nixon	**(e)** The New Nationalism

13 Everyone knows the address of the White House is 1600 Pennsylvania Avenue, Washington, D.C. What was the address of the first presidential home in New York City in 1789?

14 Name the first president to receive Secret Service protection.

15 Who was Chicago's first black mayor?

16 Which president had the most congressional experience before his presidential election?

17 Here's a two-parter: (a) name the first president to appoint a black to his cabinet, and (b) name his appointee.

18 George Washington's presidential salary was $25,000 a year. The chief executive's salary has continued to increase over the years. How much does the president currently earn annually?

19 This statesman believed that the president should not receive a salary, but, instead, should be willing to serve for free. Who was he?

20 Nine presidents used the vice presidency as a stepping stone to the Oval Office. Name four of them.

21 The Taft-Hartley Act gives the president what power?

22 Only two vice presidents have ever resigned. Can you name them?

23 Who once called Martin Luther King, Jr. "the most notorious liar in the country," using his position to wiretap the phones of other civil rights leaders?

24 David Rice Atchison served as president for only one day. Who were: (a) the outgoing president, and (b) the newly-elected president?

25 Which vice president served for the shortest period of time in American history?

26 Throughout history, presidents have awarded the faithful with prestigious jobs in their administrations. What is this practice called?

27 Name the only president who had previously served as Speaker of the House.

28 Two vice presidents died in office during whose administration? For extra credit, who were they?

29 Can you name the presidential advisor who coined the term "Cold

War" in referring to U.S.-Soviet relations after World War II: (a) Bernard Baruch, (b) James B. Brady ("Diamond Jim"), or (c) Ezra Cornell?

30 What does the "S" in Harry S Truman's middle name stand for?

31 Who was the first wife of a president to be called the "First Lady"?

32 He served as President Cleveland's vice president and as postmaster general and was the grandfather of the political candidate who was twice defeated by Dwight Eisenhower. Name him.

33 At what point in his political career did Richard Nixon announce to the press, "You won't have Nixon to kick around anymore"?

34 Try another two-parter: (a) who was the first president to travel to a foreign country while in office, and (b) where did he go?

35 Twice in history the nation had three presidents during one calendar year. What were the two years, and who were the presidents?

36 Prior to taking office, twenty-four presidents were: (a) teachers, (b) attorneys, or (c) businessmen?

7

37 Name the mayor of Chicago who was the last of the political bosses, controlling that city from 1955 to 1976.

38 This Alabama governor was permanently paralyzed in an assassination attempt during his 1972 campaign for the Democratic presidential nomination. Name him.

39 Which president originated the "domino theory," the belief that communist domination could begin with the takeover of one country, and other neighboring nations would follow suit?

40 Who was the first divorced man to run for president?

41 Name the first president who was divorced.

42 Some historians argue that George Washington technically was *not* the first president of the country. Who was?

43 The first occupants of the White House after electric lights were introduced often slept with the lights on because they were afraid of the new energy source. Who was this presidential couple?

44 Whose cabinet was said to consist of "eight millionaires and a plumber"?

45 Who was the first president to name a woman to his cabinet? For extra credit, who was she?

46 Which president referred to part of the American population as "the silent majority"?

47 The U.S. Constitution did not provide for a presidential cabinet. President Washington's first cabinet had only three appointees. Name them and the departments they headed.

48 The president's cabinet now contains fourteen executive departments. Name as many of them as you can.

49 Under whose administration did every cabinet member, with the exception of one, resign?

50 Only once in the history of the United States have a nonelected president and vice president served together. Name them.

51 Keeping in mind that the Constitution limits a president to two terms, how many terms can a president serve after completing the partial term of a predecessor?

52 Which of the following is *not* a qualification for the U.S. presidency:

(a) must be at least forty years of age, (b) must have been a U.S. resident for at least fourteen years, (c) must be a "natural born" American citizen?

53 Which president was accused of being ineligible to serve as chief executive because he was not born in the United States?

54 Name the governor of Arkansas who stationed National Guardsmen outside of Little Rock Central High School in 1957 to prevent the entrance of nine black children.

55 Eight presidents died while in office. How many can you name?

56 President William McKinley was assassinated by an avowed anarchist. Who was he: (a) Bennett Tolsky, (b) Richard Samuel Petzke, or (c) Leon F. Czolgosz?

57 Republican President Ronald Reagan appointed Democrat Jeane Kirkpatrick to what post in 1981?

58 This twentieth-century politician has served as New York's secretary of state, lieutenant governor, and governor. He also gave the keynote speech at the Democratic National Convention in 1984. Name him.

59 How long a prison term did Richard Nixon serve for his role in Watergate?

60 A twentieth-century historian coined the term "imperial presidency," a concept that several presidents throughout history had seized more power than they were entitled to, upsetting the delicate balance of power among all three branches of government. Who was the historian who wrote a 1973 book about his theory?

61 This scholar of the American presidency conducted a poll of fellow historians in 1962 evaluating thirty-one presidents. Five presidents came out on top with ratings of "great." For a two-parter: (a) who was the historian, and (b) who were the "great" presidents?

62 Here's a follow-up question. In that same survey of seventy-five historians, which two presidents up to 1962 were considered "failures?"

63 What was the "smoking gun" that brought about Richard Nixon's downfall during the Watergate investigation?

64 Who was the only president who made no major decisions while in office?

65 Which president is known for having had an unofficial "kitchen cabinet"—a group of close advisors who supposedly had more influence on this chief executive than did the appointed department heads?

66 How many vice presidents have been impeached throughout the history of the United States?

67 Which president had two assassination attempts made on his life in a period of seventeen days?

68 We all know that the president lives in the White House, but where does the vice president reside?

69 Who was the first vice president to become acting president when the chief executive was disabled?

70 This vice president viewed the presidency almost as royalty and was delighted with the Senate committee proposal that the chief executive be addressed as "His Highness, the President of the United States and Protector of Their Liberties." Who was he?

71 Who was the United States' first woman ambassador?

72 Which First Lady helped run the country when her husband suffered a paralyzing stroke, deciding which problems and issues should be brought to his bedside?

73 Why was the number "8" significant to President Martin Van Buren?

74 Name the state department official who was convicted of perjury in 1950 after being accused by former Soviet agent Whittaker Chambers of providing secret government documents to the Soviet Union.

75 On the same day in history, July 4, 1826, the fiftieth anniversary of the Declaration of Independence, two of its signers died. Who were they?

76 After serving as president, most former chief executives retire and write their memoirs. But two early presidents actually jumped over to another branch of government—the legislature. For a two-parter: (a) which nineteenth-century president became a senator, and (b) which one became a member of the House of Representatives?

77 What childhood actress later became the country's first woman chief of protocol?

78 Who was the first United States governor to be impeached, tried, and found guilty: (a) Governor Gifford Pinchot of Pennsylvania, (b) Governor William Holden of North Carolina, or (c) Governor Bob Graham of Florida?

79 Who was the only president to be married in the White House?

80 Who is a "heartbeat away from the president"?

81 Giuseppe Zangara died on the electric chair for attempting to assassinate what president-elect?

82 The election of President Abraham Lincoln in 1860 prompted the secession of eleven Southern states. Name the first state to leave the Union.

83 Who was the only president who served on the U.S. Supreme Court after being president?

84 Name the president famous for this campaign pledge: "Read my lips. No new taxes."

Answers

① Grover Cleveland. He served from 1885 to 1889 and 1893 to 1897. Benjamin Harrison defeated him in the election of 1888.

② Andrew Johnson. He violated the Tenure of Office Act by firing Edwin M. Stanton without Senate approval. He was impeached for committing "high crimes and misdemeanors," but avoided the necessary two-thirds vote for conviction by only one vote.

③ Executive privilege. The act of refusing to provide Congress with information has been around since the days of Washing-

ton, but the actual phrase "executive privilege" is a modern term.

④ *Ronald Reagan.*

⑤ *Grover Cleveland's daughter, Ruth. The news media referred to her as Baby Ruth. She died suddenly at the age of twelve from diphtheria.*

⑥ *The Brain Trust. The group got its name from the intellectual stature of its members, many of whom were Columbia University professors.*

⑦ *Speaker of the House— then president* pro tempore *of the Senate, then secretary of state, secretary of the treasury, and the other cabinet officers in the order of the creation of their department.*

⑧ *Shangri-la, so named during Franklin Delano Roosevelt's administration for James Hilton's fictitious Himalayan retreat in* Lost Horizons.

⑨ *Edward Koch.*

⑩ *William Howard Taft. After the U.S. acquired the Philippines in the Spanish-American War, Taft was President McKinley's choice to set up a civil government. He turned down two opportunities to take a seat on the Supreme Court in order to oversee this endeavor.*

⑪ *Gifford Pinchot. The Pinchots' family dog, Pep, must have temporarily lost his head when he killed Mrs. Pinchot's cat. An infuriated Pinchot put Pep on trial for murder and handed him a life sentence in the state pen. But Pep didn't serve hard time, and he became the pal of the other prisoners. He died of old age in prison after serving six years.*

⑫ *1(c), 2(e), 3(d), 4(b), 5(a).*

⑬ *Number One, Cherry Street was the first presidential address.*

⑭ *Teddy Roosevelt. The Secret Service was created in 1865 to investigate counterfeiting of currency. It took on the added responsibility of protecting the president after the assassination of President McKinley in 1901.*

⑮ *Harold Washington. After his death in 1987, Chicago's black and white aldermen fought for power. Richard M. Daley, son of former Chicago mayor Richard Daley, won the election.*

⑯ *Lyndon B. Johnson: twelve years in the House of Representatives and twelve years in the Senate.*

⑰ *(a) Lyndon B. Johnson. (b) He appointed Robert C. Weaver to his cabinet.*

He was the first black cabinet member, and also the first secretary of housing and urban development.

(18) *Two hundred thousand dollars. It was increased to that level in 1969. In addition to the salary, the president receives a $50,000 expense allowance, plus expenses for travel, staff, and maintenance of the White House. After leaving office, the president is entitled to a pension of close to $100,000 annually, secretarial staff and office space, as well as free mailing privileges.*

(19) *Benjamin Franklin.*

(20) *John Adams, Thomas Jefferson, Martin Van Buren, Theodore Roosevelt, Calvin Coolidge, Harry Truman, Lyndon B. Johnson, Richard Nixon, and George Bush.*

(21) *The power to delay a labor strike for eighty days if national health or safety are threatened. The Taft-Hartley Act was enacted, in part, to prevent abuses by labor unions against employers.*

(22) *John C. Calhoun stepped down in 1832 to lead the South's states-rights campaign as a South Carolina senator. Spiro Agnew resigned in 1973 to avoid prosecution for bribery.*

(23) *J. Edgar Hoover. It was also revealed after his death that the FBI director had improperly collected information on congressmen and presidents.*

SOMEHOW, I THINK "HAIL TO THE CHIEF" MIGHT BE INAPPROPRIATE AT THE MOMENT.

24 (a) President James Polk's term had ended on a Sunday, but (b) incoming President Zachary Taylor wanted to wait until Monday to be inaugurated. The country had to have a president during that one day, so Atchison, as president pro tempore of the Senate, was next in line to fill the spot. Atchison will be remembered for nothing in his short term in the presidency—he slept the entire day.

25 John Tyler, thirty-one days. President William Henry Harrison died one

month after his inauguration, promoting Tyler to the presidency and leaving the vice presidency vacant for the longest period of time in history.

㉖ *The "spoils," or patronage system. The Civil Service Commission and the concept of the Merit System were created to prevent the practice, but it still continues today.*

㉗ *James Polk.*

㉘ *James Madison. Vice president George Clinton died in 1812, and Elbridge Gerry died in 1814.*

㉙ *(a) Bernard Baruch. He used the term in 1947 when speaking to the South Carolina legislature. "Let us not be deceived, we are today in the midst of a Cold War. Our enemies are to be found abroad and at home."*

㉚ *Nothing. He had no middle name. And he did not use a period after the "S".*

㉛ *Lucy Hayes, wife of Rutherford B. Hayes, the nineteenth president (1877-81).*

㉜ *Adlai Ewing Stevenson. He ran again for the vice presidency in 1900, sharing the ticket with William Jennings Bryan.*

㉝ *After his gubernatorial defeat in California in November 1962.*

34 *(a) Theodore Roosevelt. (b) He went to Panama to check on the progress of the construction of the Panama Canal.*

35 *1841: Martin Van Buren, William Henry Harrison, and John Tyler. Van Buren was the outgoing president; Tyler became president when Harrison died soon after his inauguration. 1881: Rutherford B. Hayes, James A. Garfield, and Chester A. Arthur. Hayes was the outgoing president; Arthur became president when Garfield was assassinated soon after his inauguration.*

36 *(b) They were attorneys prior to taking office.*

37 *Richard J. Daley. He was the father of Richard M. Daley, elected as Chicago's mayor in 1989.*

38 *George Wallace. Despite the severe injuries inflicted by Arthur Bremer, Wallace was reelected in 1974 as Alabama's governor. In 1982 he was again elected governor, campaigning from a wheelchair. He retired in 1987 because of poor health.*

39 *Dwight Eisenhower. He was applying the domino theory to potential Communist domination in Southeast Asia.*

40 *James Cox in 1920. He remarried in 1917. His marital life did not affect his political career.*

④ *Ronald Reagan. His first wife was actress Jane Wyman.*

④ *Maryland statesman John Hanson. The Continental Congress elected him to the position of President of the Confederation, a job that provided few duties and little power. He served only one year because of poor health, and six other men filled that position before the U.S. Constitution created the actual office of President of the United States.*

④ *Benjamin and Caroline Scott Harrison (1889–93).*

④ *Dwight Eisenhower. He was criticized by his political foes for leaning heavily toward businessmen in recruiting cabinet members. The plumber reference was made regarding Eisenhower's selection of Martin Durkin, leader of a plumbers' union, for the post of secretary of labor.*

④ *Franklin D. Roosevelt, Frances Perkins. She was appointed secretary of labor in 1933 and served until his death in 1945. While she was in office, the Social Security system was created and legislation dealing with child labor, minimum wage, and workers' compensation was initiated.*

④ *Richard Nixon. During a nationally televised speech in 1969, the president attempted to trivialize the importance of Vietnam demonstrators by referring to the "silent majority" who, he said, represented the true attitude of the country by supporting the war.*

(47) *The secretary of state, Thomas Jefferson; the secretary of the treasury, Alexander Hamilton; the secretary of war, Henry Knox.*

(48) *In the sequence in which they were created, they are the departments of state, treasury, defense, interior, agriculture, justice, commerce, labor, health and human services, housing and urban development, transportation, energy, education, and veterans affairs.*

(49) *John Tyler. He refused to sign bills creating a national bank, angering members of his own Whig party. Except for Secretary of State Daniel Webster, all members of Tyler's cabinet resigned in protest in 1841.*

(50) *President Gerald Ford and Vice President Nelson Rockefeller. After Spiro Agnew resigned the vice presidency in 1973, Nixon appointed Gerald Ford to fill the spot. Nixon then resigned in 1974, moving Ford up to the presidency and giving him the opportunity to appoint Nelson Rockefeller as vice president.*

(51) *A president serving more than two years of a predecessor's term is limited to only one elected term.*

(52) *(a) The president must be at least thirty-five years of age. The youngest president was Theodore Roosevelt who was forty-two when he became president after McKinley's assassination.*

(53) *Chester Arthur. He maintained he was born in Vermont, but political rivals claimed his birthplace was Canada.*

(54) *Governor Orval Faubus attempted to block the integration of the Arkansas high school.*

(55) *William Henry Harrison, Zachary Taylor, Abraham Lincoln, James Garfield, William McKinley, Warren Harding, Franklin D. Roosevelt, and John F. Kennedy.*

(56) *(c) Leon F. Czolgosz. He said he killed the president because McKinley was an enemy of the working people. A jury deliberated only thirty-four minutes before sentencing him to death.*

(57) *Ambassador to the United Nations. She was formerly a professor of political science at Georgetown University. In 1985 she left the U.N., joined the Republican party, and returned to teaching.*

(58) *Mario Cuomo.*

(59) *None. President Ford*

pardoned Nixon one month after he resigned, although he had said he would not do so.

①⑧ *Arthur Schlesinger, Jr. He claimed that Franklin D. Roosevelt, Harry Truman, Dwight D. Eisenhower, John F. Kennedy, Lyndon B. Johnson, and Richard Nixon were those who raised the presidency to an "imperial" level by the power they usurped from the other branches.*

①⑨ *(a) Arthur Schlesinger, Sr. (b) Abraham Lincoln, George Washington, Franklin D. Roosevelt, Woodrow Wilson, and Thomas Jefferson.*

①⑩ *Ulysses S. Grant and Warren Harding were considered failures.*

①⑪ *An audiotape dated June 23, 1972. The tape revealed that the president, in a conversation with H. R. Haldeman, was supporting an effort to block the FBI investigation.*

①⑫ *William Henry Harrison. Since he died only thirty-one days after his inauguration, and all those days were spent in illness, he did not have a chance to do anything noteworthy.*

①⑬ *Andrew Jackson. The kitchen cabinet was comprised of two editors and three lower level officials in the Treasury Department. "Kitchen cabinet" was a derogatory term, referring to the backwoods manners of both President Jackson and his close advisors.*

㊞ *None. Many people believe Spiro Agnew was impeached. However, he, like Richard Nixon, had the good sense to call it quits before Congress did it for them.*

㊞ *President Gerald Ford. Lynette "Squeaky" Fromme and Sara Jane Moore were the two would-be assassins.*

㊞ *Home to the vice president is a thirty-three room mansion at the Naval Observatory in Washington.*

㊞ *George Bush. When President Reagan had surgery in 1985, Bush was president for approximately eight hours.*

㊞ *John Adams. The proposal was, of course, rejected by Congress.*

㊞ *Ruth Bryan Owen. Franklin D. Roosevelt named her minister to Denmark. She was the daughter of William Jennings Bryan.*

㊞ *Edith Galt Wilson. Without letting the American people know the seriousness of President Wilson's disability, Mrs. Wilson helped run the government for eighteen months, from September 1919 until the end of his term, screening everything that was presented to him.*

㊞ *He was the country's eighth vice president and the eighth president.*

(74) *Alger Hiss. After Chambers accused him of selling out to the Soviets, Hiss denied the charges before a federal grand jury and later sued Chambers for libel. Richard Nixon, then a congressman from California, turned the probe into a political issue, charging that President Truman was attempting to conceal the truth.*

(75) *Thomas Jefferson and John Adams. They were the only two signers of the Declaration of Independence to become president.*

(76) *(a) Andrew Johnson served in the Senate for a few months in 1875 before dying. (b) John Quincy Adams served in the House of Representatives from 1831 to 1848.*

(77) *Shirley Temple Black. She ran unsuccessfully for Congress in 1967 and was later named U.S. Ambassador to Ghana by President Nixon.*

(78) *(b) Governor William Holden. The North Carolina state legislature removed him from office after finding him guilty of "high crimes and misdemeanors" in 1870.*

(79) *Grover Cleveland. Only the second bachelor to become president, he married Frances Folsom, twenty-seven years his junior, in 1886.*

⑧⓪ *The vice president. The phrase has been used throughout history to draw attention to the importance of the vice presidential candidate. It was used in the 1988 election when Democrats tried to focus on Republican vice presidential candidate Dan Quayle, reminding voters that he could possibly ascend to the presidency should Bush die or become incapacitated.*

⑧① *Franklin Delano Roosevelt. Chicago Mayor Anton Cermak was killed during the assassination attempt. Zangara, an out-of-work bricklayer, said, "I don't hate Mr. Roosevelt personally. I hate all officials and everybody who is rich."*

⑧② *South Carolina.*

⑧③ *William Howard Taft. Justice Louis Brandeis once said of Taft," It's very difficult for me to understand how a man who is so good as Chief Justice could have been so bad as president."*

⑧④ *George Bush. His pledge to freeze taxes helped him win the presidency in 1988, but he failed to make it halfway through his term before breaking that promise (he introduced new taxes in 1990).*

The Lawmakers
on Capitol Hill

Mark Twain was rather critical of the legislative branch of government saying, "It is the will of God that we have congressmen, and we must bear the burden."

But congressmen, both representatives and senators, carry the burden of creating and passing the legislation that governs the country, as well as the added task of running for reelection every two or six years. Let's see how well you do with questions about Congress and how the U.S. legislative branch works.

❶ Let's start with a twoparter. (a) In 1982 the Equal Rights Amendment fell short of ratification by how many votes?

(b) Had it passed, what amendment number would it have been?

❷ When the Twenty-sixth Amendment to the Constitution was ratified in 1971, it guaranteed the right to vote to what group of citizens?

❸ What is the name of the California legislation passed in 1978 restricting property taxes in that state and beginning a tax reform movement across the entire country?

❹ The Mann Act was passed in 1910 to prohibit what growing practice?

❺ Name the congress-man from Ohio who was the father of one president and son of another.

❻ What position in the House of Representatives has its occupant serving as both the presiding officer and the majority party's leader?

❼ What are the assis-tants to the majority and minority floor leaders called?

❽ Name the senator who served as Chairman of the Committee on Foreign Relations in 1979 and is best known for his part in investigating charges of power abuses against the CIA.

9 In 1963 and 1964 the country had no vice president. Had President Lyndon B. Johnson died, been impeached, or become incapacitated, who would have become president?

10 Two questions in one: How many members are there (a) in the U.S. Senate, and (b) in the U.S. House of Representatives?

11 A thirty-nine-year-old congressman wants to become a U.S. senator. Is he old enough?

12 True or false. Members of both the U.S. House of Representatives and Senate must be born in the United States.

13 How long is each Senate term and the term for each member of the House of Representatives?

14 What is the limit members of Congress may serve?

15 A conservative New York congressman made a name for himself during the Reagan administration for co-sponsoring a tax cutting bill with Senator William Roth of Delaware. The former quarterback for the San Diego Chargers and the Buffalo Bills was often compared to John F. Kennedy because of his clean-cut and boyish appearance. Name him.

16 Who was the civil rights activist who was denied his elected spot in the Georgia House of Representatives because of his outspoken anti-Vietnam War views?

17 Senator Strom Thurmond holds the filibustering record in the Senate for his 1957 attempt to block the passage of the Civil Rights Act. How long did he speak: (a) 24 hours, 18 minutes, (b) 32 hours, 10 minutes, or (c) 40 hours, 2 minutes?

18 The portraits of five senators hang in the reception room of the Senate Chamber in the Capitol. Name the senators, chosen because they "left a permanent mark on our nation's history and brought distinction to the Senate."

19 What U.S. congressman holds the record for serving the longest as Speaker of the House?

20 Who chooses the Speaker of the House?

21 The first Speaker of the House, Frederick Muhlenberg, was paid twelve dollars each day that Congress was in session. In 1816 the House voted to award an annual salary of $3,000 instead. How much was the Speaker of the House earning in 1990, seventy-four years later: (a) $42,000, (b) $98,000, or (c) $115,000?

22 In which of the two bodies, House or Senate, must revenue (tax-raising) bills be introduced first?

23 How can Congress override a president's veto?

24 Name the U.S. senator from North Carolina who won national fame when he served as chairman of the Senate Watergate hearings.

25 In 1950 a well-known senatorial candidate lost the election partly because his opponent, George Smathers, announced to the world that his foe's sister was a "thespian," his brother was a "practicing homo sapiens," and that he had openly "matriculated." Name the candidate who was the victim of dirty politics in a constituency that needed to brush up on its vocabulary.

26 Who was the first woman elected to the U.S. House of Representatives?

27 Name the former professional basketball player who was elected U.S. senator from New Jersey in 1978.

28 Who was the first black woman to be elected to the U.S. House of Representatives: (a) Margaret Chase Smith, (b) Shirley Chisolm, or (c) Barbara Jordan?

29 Which chamber has the power to ratify treaties?

30 Both Ted Kennedy and his brother Robert were U.S. senators, but from different states. What state did they each represent?

31 Name the Democratic U.S. senator from New York who was formerly a presidential adviser to John F. Kennedy, Lyndon B. Johnson, and Richard Nixon, as well as ambassador to India and the U.S. representative to the United Nations.

32 Congress must convene on what day and time each year?

33 How many times a year is Congress required to meet?

34 Who was the U.S. senator from South Dakota who ran against Richard Nixon in the presidential election of 1972?

35 What state was the first to ratify the Constitution in 1787?

36 Which amendment gives the Congress the right to levy a federal income tax?

37 On March 23, 1971, residents of the nation's capital went to the polls to elect their first non-voting U.S. Representative in a century. Who was he?

38 In 1964 Congress gave President Lyndon Johnson the power to defend against North Vietnamese aggression in an area in the South China Sea. What is the name of the resolution granting this power?

39 Who was the first black U.S. senator?

40 On March 1, 1954, five congressmen were gunned down on the floor of the House chamber. Who were the would-be assassins?

41 What Atlantan was the South's first Reconstruction black congressman?

42 Who was the father of Democratic senator John Tunney from California?

43 This eloquent senator from Illinois served from 1951 to 1969, holding positions of Republican Whip and minority leader. He was significantly involved in the drafting of the

Civil Rights Act of 1964 and the Voting Rights Act of 1965. Name him.

44 To select an architect to design the Capitol in 1792, a contest was held with five hundred dollars and a plot of land as the top prize. Whose design was selected: (a) James Hoban, (b) Stephen Hallet, or (c) William Thornton?

45 The grounds of the Capitol were landscaped by the same gentleman who designed New York City's Central Park. Was he: (a) Frederick Law Olmsted, (b) Thomas Randolph Humphries, or (c) Cicero Bennett?

46 This four-term woman senator spoke out against Senator Joseph McCarthy's "red scare"—not a popular position to take at the time. Name her.

47 What is the phrase in Article II of the U.S. Constitution that gives the Senate the right to serve as a check on the president's treaty-making and appointment powers? (Hint: Allen Drury wrote a novel with a similar phrase as the title in 1959.)

48 One of the country's most animated Speakers of the House was better known by his nickname, borrowed from a professional baseball player. Can you name him?

49 How many presidents previously served in Congress?

50 Who was the U.S. representative from Connecticut from 1943 to 1947 who was also a playwright and a diplomat?

51 When did Congress pass the Seventeenth Amendment, calling for the direct election of senators rather than giving state legislatures the power to select them?

52 The Government Printing Office publishes a daily transcript of the congressional proceedings. What is the publication called?

53 Who was the president who had previously served as Senate minority leader from 1953 to 1955 and majority leader from 1955 to 1961?

54 A noted congressman during Reconstruction, who was a strong abolitionist, introduced the resolution calling for the impeachment of President Andrew Johnson. Name him.

55 Who became majority leader in the U.S. Senate when Lyndon B. Johnson became vice president, going on to hold the record for the most years in that position?

56 Name the former U.S. senator from Tennessee who was the contender for the Republican presidential nomination in 1980 and who succeeded Donald Regan as White House Chief of Staff in 1987.

57 What mechanism was used to silence the filibustering of southern senators during debates of the Civil Rights Act of 1964?

58 Who was the senator from Wisconsin who said, "I have here in my hand a list of 205 names that were known to the Secretary of State as being members of the Communist party and who nevertheless are still working and shaping policy in the state department"?

59 In 1985 President Reagan signed legislation that provided for automatic budget cuts if Congress failed to deal with the federal deficit. Name the legislation.

60 Some states still have laws on their books that prohibit retail stores from conducting business on Sunday, out of respect for the Sabbath. What are those laws called?

61 Let's see how well you know legislative terminology. Match the word or phrase in one column with its definition in the other.

Word/Phrase	Definition
1. caucus	**(a)** When a congressional committee refuses to vote on passing a bill on to the full House or Senate, thus killing it.
2. porkbarrel	**(b)** Exemption of a category of individuals from requiring compliance with a new law or regulation.
3. pigeonholing	**(c)** Officeholder having lessened power or status because his/her term is soon to end.
4. ombudsman	**(d)** Person or bureau that serves as a problem solver or mediator between citizens and government.
5. grandfather clause	**(e)** Funding that displays favoritism for a project in a legislator's home district.
6. lame duck	**(f)** Meeting to choose delegates for a nominating convention.

62 In even-numbered years why does Congress usually adjourn in early summer rather than July 31?

40

Answers

⓵ (a) 3. (b) The Twenty-seventh Amendment.

⓶ Eighteen-year-olds.

⓷ Proposition 13. An annual ceiling of one percent of the assessed value was placed on property taxes.

⓸ Prostitution. Named after U.S. congressman James Robert Mann, the White Slave Traffic Act of 1910 prohibited the transportation of women across state and international lines for immoral purposes.

⓹ John Harrison. He was the father of Benjamin Harrison and the son of William Henry Harrison. In addition to his stature as a congressman and his family name, John Harrison also gained further attention after his death when his body was snatched from his grave and turned up as a cadaver at the Ohio Medical College.

⓺ Speaker of the House.

⓻ Whips.

⓼ Frank Church. Church's committee concluded in 1975 that the CIA had been involved or supported the assassinations or coups of Fidel Castro of Cuba, Rafael Trujillo of the Dominican Republic, and the Congo's Premier Pa-

trice Lumumba. Congress created a special watchdog panel to prevent further abuses.

⑨ *Carl Albert, Speaker of the House. In 1967 the Twenty-fifth Amendment was passed, stipulating that "whenever there is a vacancy in the office of Vice President, the President shall nominate a Vice President who shall take office upon confirmation by a majority vote of both houses of Congress."*

⑩ *(a) The Senate has 100 members (two from each state), and (b) the House of Representatives has 435.*

⑪ *Yes. As specified in the Constitution, to become a member of the Senate, the candidate must be at least thirty years old. To be a member of the U.S. House of Representatives, he or she must be at least twenty-five years old.*

⑫ *False. A senator is required to have been a U.S. citizen at least nine years and a representative at least seven years. The president, of course, must be native-born.*

⑬ *A senator's term is six years, while a representative's is two.*

⑭ *Members of Congress are not limited as to how many terms they may serve, but imposing such a limit has often been suggested and debated.*

⑮ *Jack Kemp. He was co-sponsor of the bill that became the foundation of the Economic Recovery Act (1981). The act reduced individual income tax rates by twenty-five percent over three years. It reflected Kemp's support of supply-side economics, the theory that lower taxes stimulate savings and investments.*

⑯ *Julian Bond. He was the communications director of the Student Non-Violent Coordinating Committee (SNCC) from 1961 to 1965. Georgia's legislators voted 184 to 12 against admitting him as a representative in 1966. He ran twice in February and November 1966, winning both times; but on both occasions the legislature voted against him. In December 1966 the U.S. Supreme Court ruled that the legislators' actions were unconstitutional, and Bond became a member of the Georgia House in January 1967.*

⑰ *(a) Senator Strom Thurmond filibustered for 24 hours, 18 minutes.*

⑱ *Henry Clay, Robert LaFollette, Robert Taft, Daniel Webster, and John C. Calhoun.*

⑲ *Sam Rayburn. A Texas Democrat, he was Speaker for seventeen years before dying of cancer on November 16, 1961.*

⑳ *Members of the majority party choose the Speaker of the House.*

㉑ *(c) $115,000. A member of Congress, both House and Senate, received $89,500 in 1990, plus expenses for office, staff salaries, and travel.*

㉒ *Revenue bills must first be introduced in the House of Representatives.*

㉓ *A two-thirds vote by both the House and Senate can override a president's veto.*

㉔ *Sam Ervin. The Senate Watergate hearings threw this witty, yet self-proclaimed "poor ol' country lawyer" into the public spotlight. Co-chairman Senator Howard Baker said of Ervin, "Sam is the only man I know who can read the transcript of a telephone conversation and make it sound like the King James Version of the New Testament."*

㉕ *Senator Claude Pepper of Florida was the victim of dirty politics.*

㉖ *Republican Jeannette Rankin of Montana in 1916. She served from 1917 to 1919, then from 1941 to 1943. This was quite a victory for Rankin, not only because she was a woman, but because her home state of Montana voted for Democratic president Wilson in the presidential race.*

㉗ *Bill Bradley. He played for the New York Knicks from 1967 to 1977.*

(28) *(b) Shirley Chisholm. Serving from 1969 to 1983 in the U.S. House of Representatives, she was an outspoken opponent of the Vietnam War and an advocate for the indigent.*

(29) *The Senate. Treaties require a two-thirds Senate vote of approval for ratification.*

(30) *Ted Kennedy became a U.S. senator in 1962 from the state of Massachusetts. Robert Kennedy, representing the state of New York, served in the Senate from 1964 until his assassination in 1968.*

(31) *Daniel Patrick Moynihan. He is also a writer, co-author with Nathan Glazer of* Beyond the Melting Pot, *published in 1963.*

(32) *The Twentieth Amendment requires that Congress convene at noon on January 3.*

(33) *The Constitution requires that Congress meet at least once a year.*

(34) *George McGovern. A strong opponent of the Vietnam War, he served in the U.S. Senate from 1963 to 1981.*

(35) *Delaware. (Its auto licence plates proclaim it "The First State.") Nine states were required to ratify the Constitution and New Hampshire was the ninth.*

⊛ *The Sixteenth Amendment, passed in 1913, gives Congress the right to levy a federal income tax.*

㊲ *Walter Fauntroy. Congress voted in 1970 to allow District of Columbia residents to send a delegate to the U.S. House of Representatives, the first since 1875. The delegate may cast votes in committees, but not during House votes. A 1978 constitutional amendment to grant Washington voting delegates failed ratification by the required number of states in a seven-year period.*

㊳ *The Gulf of Tonkin Resolution, also called the Southeast Asia Resolution. President Johnson called on Congress to provide him with the power to respond to a Vietnamese attack on U.S. destroyers that had presumably occurred in the Gulf. The resolution was repealed in 1970.*

㊴ *Hiram R. Revels of Mississippi. He served only one year, filling the unexpired term of Jefferson Davis.*

㊵ *Four Puerto Rican terrorists. They were nationalists demanding the independence of Puerto Rico. The three men and one woman were sentenced to maximum prison terms for their actions.*

㊶ *Andrew Young. He was elected to Congress in 1972 and appointed by President Carter as the first black U.S. delegate to the*

United Nations. He was later elected as mayor of Atlanta in 1981 but lost a gubernatorial bid in 1990.

42 *Gene Tunney, who became the heavyweight boxing champion in 1926 by defeating Jack Dempsey, and then successfully defended the title in 1927.*

43 *Everett McKinley Dirksen. In addition to serving eighteen years in the Senate, Dirksen had previously served sixteen years in the House of Representatives.*

44 *(c) William Thornton. He was a doctor who was permitted to submit his entry after the deadline. The building was designed as a home for Congress, the Library of Congress, and the Supreme Court. The runnerup, Stephen Hallet, was given $500 and was put in charge of overseeing the Capitol's construction. James Hoban designed the president's house.*

45 *(a) Frederick Law Olmsted landscaped the grounds of the Capitol.*

46 *Margaret Chase Smith, Republican from Maine.*

47 *Advice and Consent. (Drury's book was entitled* Advise and Consent.*)*

48 *Thomas "Tip" O'Neill served as House Speaker from 1977 to 1987. He got his nickname "Tip" from St. Louis Brown's ball-*

player James Edward O'Neill, who made a name for himself by his ability to get walked to first base by tipping off foul balls.

㊾ *Twenty-two.*

㊿ *Clare Booth Luce. She wrote several plays, including* The Women *(1936). She was also the U.S. Ambassador to Italy from 1953 to 1956. Luce was married to the publisher who created* Time *magazine in 1923, Henry Robinson Luce.*

(51) *1913.*

(52) The Congressional Record. *House and Senate members are allowed to revise their remarks or add new comments before the* Record *is printed.*

(53) *Lyndon B. Johnson.*

(54) *Thaddeus Stevens.*

(55) *Mike Mansfield. He served sixteen years as majority leader in the U.S. Senate.*

(56) *Howard Baker. He gained national attention while serving on the Senate committee investigating Watergate.*

(57) *Cloture. Filibustering, unlimited debate on a bill in the Senate, can be ended through a cloture vote. When it was introduced in 1917, cloture required a two-thirds major-*

ity vote, but was revised in 1975 to make it easier to invoke, with only a three-fifths majority of Senate membership necessary.

(58) Senator Joseph McCarthy. This speech in February of 1950 was the beginning of his communist "witch hunt" that touched not only political adversaries, but writers and entertainers as well. In December 1954, the Senate "condemned" him for his groundless four-year anti-communist crusade.

(59) The Gramm-Rudman Act was passed to deal with the federal deficit.

(60) Blue laws. The name came from the blue paper they were often printed on in the 1600s.

(61) 1(f), 2(e), 3(a), 4(d), 5(b), 6(c).

(62) To give senators and representatives time to campaign for reelection.

The U.S.
Supreme Court

*C*ongress can pass
legislation, the president can sign it, but
only the Supreme Court has the power
to determine the law's constitutionality
and how it should be applied. Here's a
chance to see how much you know about
famous jurists, some of the more impor-
tant Supreme Court cases, and how the
court system works in the United States.

❶ Who was the first
chief justice of the United States?

❷ In 1987 the U.S. Sen-
ate rejected President Reagan's first two nomina-
tions to fill an associate justice position on the U.S.
Supreme Court. For a two-parter: (a) who were the
first two people nominated, and (b) who was ultimately approved to fill the vacancy?

③ The ethical as well as political issue of "death with dignity" and the right to die was brought to the attention of the nation with what well-known case in 1975?

④ Name the United States Supreme Court chief justice who earned the title of the "Great Dissenter."

⑤ Who was the first attorney general of the United States: (a) Oliver Ellsworth, (b) Edmund Randolf, or (c) John Blair?

⑥ How many justices sit on the United States Supreme Court?

⑦ How long is the term of a United States Supreme Court justice?

⑧ In which landmark case did the United States Supreme Court decide that poor people were entitled to free legal counsel if charged with a criminal offense: (a) *Gibbons v. Ogden*, (b) *Gideon v. Wainwright*, or (c) *McCulloch v. Madison*?

⑨ Which twentieth-century president was accused of "court packing" when he suggested that he be given the power to appoint up to six additional Supreme Court justices if those over the age of seventy refused to step down?

10 Roger B. Taney's appointment to the Supreme Court by President Andrew Jackson in 1836 was a first. What first was it?

11 Because of the ever-increasing caseload, the U.S. Supreme Court set a time limit for oral arguments by attorneys. How much time is each side permitted?

12 Name the 1973 landmark case that gave women the right to have an abortion during the first three months of pregnancy.

13 On September 25, 1981, the first woman justice on the U.S. Supreme Court was sworn in. For a two-parter: (a) who was she, and (b) whose seat did she fill?

14 What does the term "Rule of Four" mean in the Supreme Court?

15 This major decision, handed down in 1803, introduced the doctrine of judicial review, giving the Supreme Court the right to review legislation to determine if Congress had overstepped its constitutional boundaries. Was it: (a) *Fletcher v. Peck*, (b) *Marbury v. Madison,* or (c) *Gideon v. Wainwright*?

16 In what year were women first permitted to argue cases before the U.S. Supreme Court?

17 Throughout history, the United States government has been one of the most prominent parties to lawsuits heard before the U.S. Supreme Court. Which of the following represents the United States in Court: (a) the attorney general, (b) the solicitor general, or (c) the barrister general?

18 Name the day of the week and month of the year in which the U.S. Supreme Court convenes.

19 Which justice was threatened with impeachment not once but twice?

20 Who was the first U.S. Supreme Court associate justice to resign his seat under the threat of impeachment?

21 Only once has a Supreme Court justice been impeached. Who was he?

22 What occupations did justices Earl Warren and Charles Evans Hughes both have just prior to their appointments to the Supreme Court?

23 What famous lawyer represented Captain Ernest Medina, the company commander who supposedly gave the orders to First Lieutenant William Calley and others to wipe out the Vietnamese village of My Lai: (a) Marvin Mitchelson, (b) F. Lee Bailey, or (c) Melvin Belli?

24 Name the 1857 decision that gave the Supreme Court the appearance of being "pro-slavery," caused damage to the public's perception of the Court, and supposedly helped push the country closer to the Civil War.

25 The first important ruling by the U.S. Supreme Court was *Chisholm v. Georgia*. What issue was addressed in this 1793 decision: (a) whether Georgians had the right to own slaves, (b) whether a citizen from one state could sue another state, (c) whether a citizen could be taxed by another state?

26 What long-standing segregation policy was struck down as unconstitutional in the case of *Brown v. Board of Education*?

27 In 1979 this attorney defended Michelle Triola against actor Lee Marvin when she demanded a form of payment based on their live-in relationship, though they had never formally married. Who was the attorney? For extra credit, what did this type of payment come to be called?

28 Name the liberal chief justice who guided the Supreme Court through school desegregation, the barring of prayer in public schools, equitable legislative districts apportioned by population, and the revamping of criminal rights.

29 George Washington had the opportunity to make eleven Supreme Court appointments, primarily because he seated the original Court. Which president had the second highest number of appointments?

30 In *Furman v. Georgia* the Supreme Court threw out all death penalty statutes throughout all the states, declaring them arbitrary and in violation of due process rights. In what year was this historic decision handed down?

31 Who was the first person to be executed after the death penalty was reinstated in several states?

32 When Chief Justice Warren Burger retired in 1986, who did President Reagan select to succeed him?

33 This university received a bill for one-half million dollars in back taxes from the IRS, which charged that, because the school discriminated against blacks, it was not considered a charitable institution. The Supreme Court upheld the IRS charge in 1983. Name the university.

34 What famous lawyer represented Jack Ruby, the man who killed accused John F. Kennedy assassin, Lee Harvey Oswald?

35 What U.S. Supreme Court justice was the chief prosecutor at the Nuremberg Trials: (a) William O. Douglas, (b) Robert H. Jackson, or (c) Felix Frankfurter?

36 How many Supreme Court justices were not lawyers?

37 Who was the first black U.S. Supreme Court justice?

38 Who was the University of California applicant whose name became synonymous with the term "reverse discrimination"?

39 In 1966 the Supreme Court ruled that, upon arrest, police had to advise suspects of the right to remain silent, as well as the right to a court-appointed attorney. What are those rights known as?

40 One chief justice had the distinction of appearing on the $10,000 bill. Who is he?

41 Name the U.S. Supreme Court justice who resigned to accept the job of U.S. ambassador to the United Nations in 1965.

42 Who was the first Jewish U.S. Supreme Court justice?

43 Which U.S. Supreme Court justice was once a member of the Ku Klux Klan?

44 This defendant in the celebrated 1925 "Monkey Trial" was found guilty of teaching the theory of evolution in the public schools. For a two-parter: (a) who was he, and (b) who were the two lawyers involved in the trial?

45 Justice Tom Campbell Clark resigned in 1967 when President Johnson appointed Clark's son as attorney general. The justice felt this could be perceived as a conflict of interest if he remained on the Court. Who was his son?

46 A class action suit, brought by Vietnam war veterans against several chemical companies, was settled on May 7, 1984, for $180 million. The veterans alleged that exposure to a herbicide in Vietnam caused cancer and liver damage. What was the name of the herbicide?

47 What nationally known civic organization was ordered in 1984 by the Supreme Court to fully open its membership to women?

48 Charlotte, North Carolina, was the testing ground in the early 1970s for what political issue?

49 Which chief justice was selected to head a commission investigating the Kennedy assassination?

50 Let's test your knowledge of legal terms (and your Latin). Match the term with its definition.

Term	**Definition**
1. amicus curiae	**(a)** A law turning an innocent action into a crime after it was committed.
2. res judicata	**(b)** The policy of following principles established in previous judicial decisions.
3. ex post facto	**(c)** A writ requiring that the defendant be permitted to come before the court to hear justification of his confinement.
4. habeas corpus	**(d)** A plea of not contesting a criminal charge; treated as a guilty plea yet cannot be used as an admission in other cases.
5. nolo contendere	**(e)** A defense of not being of sound mind.
6. stare decisis	**(f)** a final judgment by a court, not subject to litigation again by the same parties.
7. tort	**(g)** A person who is not a party to a lawsuit but who requests or is asked to participate.

(*Question 50 continued on next page*)

Term	**Definition**
8. non compos mentis	**(h)** A wrong or injury against a person or property.

51 Both "libel" and "slander" deal with defamation of character, or injuring one's reputation. What is the difference between the two words?

52 Laws that perpetuated racism and discrimination throughout American history were gradually chipped away through Supreme Court decisions and legislation. What were the segregation laws called?

53 One attorney made a name for himself by prosecuting Charles Manson in the Tate-LaBianca murders and for writing a bestseller about it. For a two-parter: (a) name the lawyer, and (b) give the book title.

54 Who was the lawyer whose celebrated practice ran the gamut from defending Al Capone and other mobsters to successfully arguing a case before the Supreme Court that established the unconstitutionality of excluding blacks from the jury (the Scottsboro Boys case)?

55 In 1919 U.S. Supreme Court Justice Wendell Holmes established a test for determining when the government was unconstitutionally restricting freedom of speech. What is the famous phrase he introduced in the case of *Schenk v. United States*?

56 Another matching question. The twenty-six amendments to the U.S. Constitution provide Americans with their basic freedoms and rights. See how many of them you know by matching the amendment number with the right or privilege granted.

Amendment	**Right Granted**
1. First Amendment	(a) Guarantees against unreasonable search and seizure.
2. Second Amendment	(b) Gives women the right to vote.
3. Fourth Amendment	(c) Guarantees freedom of religion, speech, the press, assembly, and to petition the government.
4. Sixth Amendment	(d) Lowers the voting age to eighteen.
5. Eighth Amendment	(e) Prohibits slavery.
6. Thirteenth Amendment	(f) Provides for a speedy trial.
7. Ninteenth Amendment	(g) Prohibits cruel and unusual punishment.
8. Twenty-sixth Amendment	(h) Grants the right to keep and bear arms.

57 Name the system provided by the U.S. Constitution ensuring that no one branch of the government commands too much power.

58 One year after the decision in *Brown v. Board of Education*, the Supreme Court provided local school boards with guidelines on how to proceed with desegregation. What phrase did the Court use in setting up a timeframe?

59 Two Italian radicals were convicted in 1921 for theft and murder at a shoe factory in Massachusetts. The trial sparked interest across the country. Many believe that the two were convicted, not because the evidence against them was substantial, but because they were anarchists. Name them.

60 What is the more common name for the clause in the Constitution that gives Congress the power to enact all "necessary and proper" laws in order to carry out its duties?

61 What does a witness plead when he chooses not to answer because it may "tend to incriminate him"?

62 There is an amendment that protects individuals against being tried for the same offense. (a) Which amendment is it, and (b) what's the proper term for this?

63 Here's a three parter: (a) which constitutional amendment, ratified in 1919, authorized prohibition, (b) what two states failed to ratify it, and (c) which amendment repealed it?

Answers

① Chief Justice John Jay. He resigned in 1795 to serve as New York's governor.

② (a) Robert H. Bork and Douglas Ginsberg. Bork was seen as too conservative, with civil rights and other liberal organizations lobbying strenuously for Senate rejection. Ginsberg's nomination was opposed after he admitted he had smoked marijuana in his younger days. He eventually withdrew his name. (b) Anthony M. Kennedy. Prior to his appointment, he served on the U.S. Court of Appeals, Ninth Circuit.

③ The Karen Ann Quinlan case. This case prompted states to implement right-to-die legislation, allowing terminally ill individuals to execute documents instructing their doctors and families not to prolong their life with life support systems and other extraordinary measures.

④ Oliver Wendell Holmes. His liberal views on social issues often caused heated debates among the justices—thus, the "Great Dissen-

ter" epithet. He was the author of a controversial book, The Common Law, *published in 1881.*

⑤ *(b) Edmund Randolf. He took office on September 26, 1789, two days after the position was created, with a starting salary of $1500 annually.*

⑥ *Nine. The Judiciary Act, which created the Court in 1789, called for only six justices. Congress set the number of justices at nine in 1869 after the number fluctuated many times over the eighty-year period.*

⑦ *A justice is appointed for life to serve until retirement, death, or impeachment. A justice may retire with full pay after reaching the age of seventy or at sixty-five after serving fifteen years.*

⑧ *(b)* Gideon v. Wainwright *(1963). Clarence Gideon served as his own counsel because the state of Florida would not provide him free legal services.*

⑨ *Franklin D. Roosevelt. The Senate refused to go along with the president's plan, but former president Herbert Hoover and others accused him of trying to stack the Court to assure support for some of his New Deal proposals.*

⑩ *Roger B. Taney was the first Catholic appointed to the U.S. Supreme Court.*

⑪ *Thirty minutes. Oral arguments are presented on Mondays, Tuesdays, and Wednesdays for fourteen weeks during the months of October through April.*

⑫ Roe v. Wade. *In this case the court put limits on abortions during the second and third trimester.*

⑬ *(a) Sandra Day O'Connor. (b) She replaced Justice Potter Stewart, who retired in July 1981 at the age of sixty-six. The Senate confirmation of Justice O'Connor was unanimous even though, as an Arizona state senator, the judge had supported a woman's right to have an abortion.*

⑭ *Because the U.S. Supreme Court is inundated with thousands of cases each year, the justices have to determine which ones they should hear. For a case to make it before the Court, four of the nine justices have to vote in favor of hearing it. Thus, the "Rule of Four."*

⑮ *(b)* Marbury v. Madison. *This ruling was the first time the Court nullified an act of Congress.*

⑯ *1879. The women attorneys were required to have practiced at least three years in a state supreme court.*

⑰ *(b) The solicitor general. The solicitor general chooses and then argues the cases the federal government wants to bring before the Supreme Court.*

⑱ *The U.S. Supreme Court convenes on the first Monday in October.*

⑲ *William Orville Douglas. Douglas caused an uproar in 1953 when he stayed the execution of convicted Communist spies Julius and Ethel Rosenberg. An impeachment resolution was introduced but was tabled after only one day of hearings in a Senate committee. Seventeen years later, a special House subcommittee investigated several accusations made by Minority Leader Gerald Ford against Douglas, including conflict of interest charges. The subcommittee found no cause for impeachment.*

⑳ *Abe Fortas. He came under a barrage of criticism for receiving funds from a foundation established by Louis Wolfson, later convicted of securities violations.*

㉑ *Justice Samuel Chase. He was charged with making statements about government officials that were "false, scandalous, and malicious." He was acquitted in 1805.*

㉒ *Both were governors— Warren from California and Hughes from New York.*

㉓ *(b) F. Lee Bailey. He is known for many other cases including the defense of the Boston Strangler, Patty Hearst, and Dr. Sam Sheppard, an osteopath convicted of murdering his wife.*

㉔ *The Dred Scott Case.* *The Court, led by Chief Justice Taney, declared (1) that Congress did not have the right to determine whether slavery could exist in the new territories and (2) that blacks could not become American citizens.*

㉕ *(b) The Court ruled that a citizen from South Carolina had the right to sue the state of Georgia. In 1798 the Eleventh Amendment was passed to resolve this question and remedy a controversial decision by the Supreme Court.*

㉖ *Separate but Equal. This Court decision, which prohibited segregated schools in the United States, affected about eleven million students. The separate but equal doctrine had been the law of the land for fifty-eight years, since the 1896* Plessy v. Ferguson *decision.*

㉗ *Marvin Mitchelson. Triola prevailed, with the Court ordering Marvin to pay. The case made Mitchelson a hot commodity among celebrities and opened the door for others to demand "palimony"—the popular term for this court-ordered financial support. Mitchelson's popularity waned, however, when he faced charges of eth-*

ics violations from the California Bar as well as rape charges by two former clients.

(28) *Earl Warren. Appointed by President Dwight Eisenhower, he served from 1953 to 1968.*

(29) *Franklin D. Roosevelt appointed nine justices. At the time of his death, only two justices remained on the Court who had been appointed prior to his four terms as president.*

(30) *1972. In* Furman v. Georgia *the Court was not abolishing the death penalty. It ruled that state laws provided no standards for judges and juries to follow, resulting in arbitrary death sentences. The states were directed either to create clearer laws or abolish them.*

(31) *Gary Gilmore. He was executed by firing squad in Utah, January 1977, having been convicted of a double murder.*

(32) *William Hubbs Rehnquist. Having served as an assistant attorney general, he was placed on the Supreme Court by President Nixon in 1971. He became the sixteenth chief justice in 1986.*

(33) *Bob Jones University in Greenville, South Carolina. The Supreme Court disagreed with the university's argument that its First Amendment right of freedom of religion was violated, voting eight to one in favor of the IRS.*

㉞ *Melvin Belli.*

㉟ *(b) Robert H. Jackson. He took a leave of absence from the Court in 1945 to act as chief prosecutor at the Nazi trials.*

㊱ *Although not a constitutional requirement, all justices have previously been lawyers; however, not all have received degrees from law schools. Some of the earlier justices received on-the-job legal training.*

㊲ *Thurgood Marshall. Formerly U.S. solicitor general, Marshall was named an associate justice in 1967 after being nominated by President Lyndon Johnson.*

㊳ *Allan P. Bakke. In 1978 the Supreme Court ruled that Bakke, who is white, had been denied admission to the University of California Medical School at Davis because the school had a fixed quota system for admitting minorities, a system that was unconstitutional. However, while affirming the illegality of racial quotas, the Supreme Court also said, "Government may take race into account when it acts not to demean or insult any racial group but to remedy disadvantages cast on minorities by past racial prejudice."*

㊴ *Miranda warnings. Ernesto Miranda was arrested for rape and confessed without being advised of his right to counsel. The Court ruled in* Miranda v. Arizona *(1966) that the confession was not admissible.*

(40) *Chief Justice Salmon P. Chase. The honor of having his portrait on the $10,000 bill had nothing to do with his position on the high court. He was President Lincoln's secretary of the treasury, and is credited with establishing the national bank system.*

(41) *Arthur J. Goldberg. He took the U.N. spot that was left vacant after Adlai Stevenson's death.*

(42) *Louis Brandeis. A Woodrow Wilson appointee, he served from 1916 to 1939.*

(43) *Hugo Black. Ironically, Black became a leading judicial liberal.*

(44) *(a) John Scopes. At the time, Tennessee had a law against teaching Darwin's theory, a statute that was not abolished for another forty-two years. Scopes was later released on a legal technicality. The trial received national attention, not only because of the issue, but because of the dramatic presentations of (b) Clarence Darrow for the defense and William Jennings Bryan for the prosecution.*

(45) *Ramsey Clark.*

(46) *Agent Orange.*

(47) *The Jaycees in* Gomez Bethe v. U.S. Jaycees.

(48) *School integration. In*

Swann v. Charlotte-Mecklenburg County Board of Education, *the Supreme Court ruled that busing and the shifting of school district lines was acceptable in order to bring about integration of the schools.*

(49) *Earl Warren. He headed—what else?—the Warren Commission, created by President Johnson in November 1963. The commission concluded ten months later that both Lee Harvey Oswald, Kennedy's assassin, and Jack Ruby, Oswald's killer, had each acted alone. The commission's findings were extremely controversial, with many critics believing the Kennedy assassination was the result of a conspiracy.*

(50) *1(g), 2(f), 3(a), 4(c), 5(d), 6(b), 7(h), 8(e).*

(51) *"Libel" involves defamation through the written word; and "slander" is spoken.*

(52) *Jim Crow laws.*

(53) *(a) Leo Bugliosi. (b) The book is entitled* Helter Skelter. *Bugliosi was successful in prosecuting Manson and other members of his cult in 1971, but their death sentences were reduced to life in prison when capital punishment was abolished one year later.*

(54) *Samuel Leibowitz. An extremely talented litigator, he defended 140 capital cases, and only one defendant was sentenced to death.*

Ⓟ *"Clear and present danger." Schenk was charged with sedition for mailing pamphlets to military draftees, urging them to protest the "unconstitutional" draft. Holmes ruled that Schenk's leaflets created a "clear and present danger" to a nation at war.*

Ⓠ *1(c), 2(h), 3(a), 4(f), 5(g), 6(e), 7(b), 8(d).*

Ⓡ *Checks and Balances.*

Ⓢ *"With all deliberate speed." Civil rights groups were unhappy with the Court's vagueness and lack of a specific date for ending segregation.*

Ⓣ *Nicola Sacco and Bartolomeo Vanzetti. They were electrocuted in 1927.*

Ⓤ *The "necessary and proper" clause in Article I, section 8 is also called the "elastic clause."*

Ⓥ *"The Fifth." The Fifth Amendment states that an individual "shall not be compelled in any criminal case to be a witness against himself."*

Ⓦ *(a) Again, the Fifth Amendment. (b) The term is double jeopardy.*

Ⓧ *(a) The Eighteenth Amendment, (b) Connecticut and Rhode Island, (c) Twenty-first Amendment (1933).*

The Campaign Trail

The closest most Americans get to politics is the voting booth. The whole elective process begins with a politician announcing his candidacy and running a campaign leading up to election night. For the offices of the president and vice president, this includes national party conventions, as well as the formality of the inauguration. How much do you actually know about elections in our country? You might be surprised to find out!

❶ Name the only president who was inaugurated in two different cities. (Hint: Neither city was Washington, D.C.)

❷ The second inauguration speech given by the president in question 1 holds a record of sorts. What made this speech memorable?

3 What was President Calvin Coolidge's 1924 campaign slogan?

4 Which president had the distinction of being the first to arrive at his inauguration in an automobile? And, for extra credit, in what year was he inaugurated?

5 This same president had another "first." What was it?

6 What branch of the service was involved in controversy during the vice presidential campaign of Dan Quayle?

7 The Twenty-fourth Amendment eliminated an antiquated and racially discriminatory election practice. What was it?

8 Two presidential elections pitted a Quaker candidate against a Catholic. Can you name the candidates and, for extra credit, the years?

9 It took 103 ballots for the 1924 Democratic national convention to come up with a nominee. What was the problem, and who did they finally choose as their candidate?

10 Name the only state Ronald Reagan lost in the 1984 election.

11 This president's campaign manager accurately predicted that his man would get his party's nomination about eleven minutes after two A.M. on the Friday of the convention. The amazing thing about his prediction is that he made it several months *before* the convention. Who was the soon-to-be president?

12 What song did Franklin Delano Roosevelt adopt for his 1932 presidential campaign?

13 Name the president who was the object of a rumored assassination plot to be carried out in Baltimore, Maryland, en route to his inauguration in Washington, D.C.

14 Which First Lady died after her husband was elected to the presidency but before he was able to take the oath of office?

15 When women were finally given the right to vote for president, who were the two major party candidates?

16 During which election were the victorious president and vice president from different parties? For extra credit, name the two men elected.

17 In the early 1800s voting districts' boundary lines were redrawn to favor the party in power, a practice that is now illegal. What was this practice called?

18 Name the three presidents who won even though they received fewer popular votes than their closest opponent.

19 The Twentieth Amendment to the U.S. Constitution, ratified in 1933, shortened the lame duck period for a president by moving the inauguration date to January 20. What was the original inauguration date?

20 A blackout during the Republican convention of 1876 took everyone by surprise, and changed the outcome of the nominating process. Which candidate was expected to win but didn't?

21 Name the president who said during his inaugural speech, "Let us begin a new period. Let us never negotiate out of fear. But let us never fear to negotiate." Extra points: What famous phrase came from the same speech?

22 Who was given the right to vote by the Twenty-third Amendment?

23 After it entered the Union in 1912, New Mexico had the distinction of always casting its vote for the winning presidential candidate until which president?

24 Prior to the election of 1804 electors cast two votes each, not specifying which was for president and which for vice president. The highest vote-getter became the chief executive and the second highest was his vice president. What happened in the election of 1800 that made it necessary to change this method?

25 Here's a two-parter: (a) who were the candidates in the election of 1800, and (b) how was a president chosen?

26 During two Democratic conventions there was no need for a delegate vote as the nominees were selected by acclamation. What were the election years, and who were the presidential and vice presidential candidates?

27 Who won the Republican nomination in 1880 even though he was not interested in running for president?

28 Jerry Rubin, Abbie Hoffman, Tom Hayden and four other individuals were charged, but later acquitted of conspiracy to incite a riot during the 1968 Democratic national convention in Chicago. For this two-parter, give the name of (a) this group of defendants, and (b) the name of the defendant who was granted a separate trial.

29 Which presidential candidate won by a wide margin with campaign promises of "a chicken in every pot and a car in every garage"?

30 In 1924 the first women won gubernatorial races in two separate states. Who were they, and what were the states?

31 The Kennedy versus Nixon election of 1960 was one of the closest in U.S. history. Kennedy won by what percentage of the popular vote: (a) .2%, (b) 1½%, or (c) 2%?

32 Only once in history did the Senate choose the vice president. What election year was it, and who was the vice president selected?

33 Delegates to the 1972 Democratic national convention decided to have a little fun and placed the names of Mao Zedong (Mao Tse-Tung), Archie Bunker, and others into nomination as vice presidential candidates? Who "beat" the Chinese leader, television character, and other unconventional candidates for the Democratic vice presidential nomination?

34 Who lost his bid for the presidency by only one electoral vote?

35 Who was the first president to be elected to a third term?

36 Four hundred people attended the nation's first inaugural ball. Whose election were they celebrating?

37 In the election of 1864 the Democratic candidate refused to run on his party's platform. Who was he?

38 During what presidential election did the whole country begin to vote on the same designated day?

39 One president caught a cold shortly after his inauguration and died one month later. Name him.

40 When was the first time Americans could watch a presidential nominating convention on television? For extra credit, who was nominated for president?

41 Democratic congresswoman Helen Gahagan Douglas of California didn't stand a chance against the sneaky campaign tactics of her Republican opponent in the 1950 U.S. Senate race. Late in the campaign, he had pink flyers handed out accusing Ms. Douglas of having a pro-communist voting record. Who was this "smear artist"?

42 The 1984 Democratic presidential nomination aspirant was a one issue candidate, running on a ticket calling for a nuclear weapons freeze. Can you name him?

43 Who was the first black to capture one vote at a national presidential nominating convention?

44 What city has been the site of the most major political party conventions?

45 Here's a two-parter: (a) during what year did a major political party hold its first national party convention, and (b) where was it held?

46 When and where did the Republicans hold their first national convention?

47 Whose inauguration was the first to be televised?

48 Who was the first major party presidential candidate to personally accept his party's nomination at a convention?

49 A candidate from the opposition major party didn't personally accept his party's nomination until several years later. Who was it and when?

50 During which election was the first national party platform created?

51 Only one president was ever sworn in on an airplane. (a) Who was he, and (b) what were the circumstances?

52 What did Millard Fillmore and Gerald Ford have in common?

53 Presidential candidates spend millions of dollars on their campaigns, particularly since the advent of radio and tele-vision. How much did Abraham Lincoln spend on his 1860 campaign: (a) $25,000, (b) $100,000, or (c) $325,000?

54 Who was the first presidential candidate to spend more than a million dollars in his election bid?

55 One Democrat wasn't going to let one defeat, or two, or three, discourage him from winning his party's nomination and the job of chief executive. He was finally success-ful on his fourth try. Who was he?

56 For the first time in history, organized labor endorsed a presidential nominee in 1983. Who was he?

57 Prior to 1975 the only way a woman made it to the position of governor was to ride in on her husband's coattails. Who was the first woman governor elected whose husband had not previously held that office?

58 Who did Ronald Rea-gan defeat in the 1966 California gubernatorial race?

59 Name the first presi-dential candidate of the Republican party.

60 According to the 1964 Republican presidential candidate, Barry Goldwater, he chose his running mate for a particular, if unusual, reason. (a) Who was he, and (b) what was Goldwater's reason?

61 Name the only elected president who failed to be renominated by his party.

62 Who was the only president to be unanimously chosen by the Electoral College?

63 In the summer of 1984 it was said of her: "She's a woman; she's ethnic; she's Catholic." Who was she?

64 In the election of 1984 a black civil rights activist took on Walter Mondale for the Democratic nomination. Can you name him?

65 Which president ran twice for reelection and lost both times?

66 The Republicans said this Democrat was the candidate of the three "A" words: acid, abortion, and amnesty. Who was the candidate?

67 There was only one presidential candidate in the election of 1820; President James Monroe was unopposed for reelection. All but one of the 232 electors cast their vote for him, with Governor William Plumer of New Hampshire as the only holdout. For whom did he vote and why?

68 Who was the wizard who financially rehabilitated one of the country's major automobile manufacturers and whose name was mentioned as a potential Democratic presidential candidate in 1988?

69 This U.S. senator from Delaware withdrew from the Democratic presidential nominating race in 1988 after it was revealed that he had plagiarized in his political speeches and on a law school paper. Name him.

70 What is a PAC?

71 Candidates are often labeled based on their party affiliations, political leanings, and their chances of winning. See how well you can match candidate labels with their meanings.

Labels	**Meanings**
1. perennial	**(a)** favors less government control
2. hawk	**(b)** has the backing of convention delegates
3. incumbent	**(c)** persistent at running, but not successful
4. liberal	**(d)** opposes war or aggression

(*Question 71 continued on next page*)

Labels	Meanings
5. favorite son	**(e)** supports reliance on government assistance
6. dove	**(f)** presently holds the office
7. dark horse	**(g)** supports military intervention or war
8. conservative	**(h)** a long shot, not expected to win

72 During the heated presidential campaign of 1800, candidate Aaron Burr became so infuriated at one of his political opponents that he killed him in a duel. Who was he?

Answers

① *George Washington. He was inaugurated in New York City in 1789 and in Philadelphia in 1793.*

② *Washington's Philadelphia inaugural speech was the shortest in American history—only 135 words.*

③ *"Keep cool with Coolidge" was his campaign slogan in the election of 1924.*

④ *Warren G. Harding rode to his inauguration in an automobile in 1921.*

⑤ *Harding was the first president to have his inaugural address broadcast on the radio.*

⑥ *The National Guard. Quayle was accused of using influence to gain entry into the Indiana National Guard in order to avoid active combat duty during the Vietnam War. The Republicans turned the tables on the news media for their implication that joining the National Guard was less patriotic than joining any other branch of the armed services.*

⑦ *The poll tax. The tax was levied on all voters, but often prevented the poor, particularly blacks in the South, from voting. The Twenty-fourth Amendment, adopted in 1964, eliminated the poll tax in federal elections, and a 1966 Supreme Court ruling eliminated poll taxes in state and local elections.*

⑧ *In the election of 1928 Quaker Herbert Hoover ran against Catholic Al Smith. In 1960 Richard Nixon, a Quaker, took on Catholic John F. Kennedy. Each persuasion batted .500.*

⑨ *New York corporate lawyer John W. Davis of West Virginia became the nominee. There was a deadlock between two other favored candidates: William McAdoo and New York governor, Alfred E. Smith. McAdoo released his delegates after the 99th ballot, moving third place Davis into second. Smith lost ground, and Davis was finally declared the party's nominee on the 103rd ballot after nine days of voting.*

⑩ *Walter Mondale took his home state of Minnesota. He also won in the District of Columbia. Reagan won fifty-nine percent of the popular vote, and Mondale took forty-one percent.*

⑪ *Warren Harding. His campaign manager, Harry Daugherty, predicted that Harding would be selected ". . . when fifteen or twenty men, bleary-eyed and perspiring profusely from the heat, are sitting at a table, some one of them will say: 'Who will we nominate?' " He was surely psychic because the formal convention deadlocked, and the party leaders took it upon themselves to decide on a nominee in a suite at Chicago's Blackstone Hotel early Friday morning. Harding's name was suggested, and because he was a "safe" candidate, he was nominated.*

⑫ *"Happy Days Are Here Again." This song reflected Roosevelt's attitude of optimism and his hope of bringing the United States out of the Great Depression.*

⑬ *Abraham Lincoln. When Pinkerton detectives learned of the assassina-*

tion scheme, they snuck the president-to-be onto a different, heavily guarded railway car for the rest of the trip to Washington, D.C.

⑭ *Rachel Jackson. She died unexpectedly in December 1828 before Jackson was sworn in as president.*

⑮ *Republican Warren Harding and Democrat James M. Cox were the choices in the election of 1920.*

⑯ *The election of 1796. President John Adams (Federalist) and Vice President Thomas Jefferson (Democratic-Republican) were elected.*

⑰ *Gerrymandering. In 1812 Massachusetts Governor Elbridge Gerry, one of the signers of the Declaration of Independence and vice president in Madison's second administration, had his state redistricted to give the Republicans a clear advantage over the Federalists. One of the districts took on the shape of a salamander, and critics then called it a "Gerrymander."*

⑱ *John Quincy Adams (1824), Rutherford Hayes (1876), and Benjamin Harrison (1888).*

⑲ *March 4. Senator George Norris of Nebraska pushed hard for this change for several years, but it wasn't until President*

Hoover's lame duck status in 1932 interfered with handling the faltering economy that Congress decided to act.

(20) House Speaker James G. Blaine. Because Blaine had a zealous crowd of supporters at the convention, his opponents tried to adjourn the session before a vote, but they realized it would be futile. Suddenly, the room went black. The gas lines apparently had been cut, and the session had to adjourn for the day. The excited support for Blaine subsided by the next morning, and his opponents were able to shift support to Rutherford B. Hayes, who finally won on the seventh ballot.

(21) President John F. Kennedy. Perhaps even more quoted, was the phrase from the same speech, "Ask not what your country can do for you. Ask what you can do for your country."

(22) Residents of the District of Columbia. Before 1961 they did not have the right to vote in presidential elections. Since the majority of Washington's residents were black, their disenfranchisement brought accusations of racial discrimination.

(23) Gerald Ford in 1976. The state of New Mexico could have held their record had they supported Jimmy Carter.

㉔ *The top two candidates received the same number of electoral votes.*

㉕ *Thomas Jefferson, Aaron Burr, and John Adams. Burr tied Jefferson, forcing the House to break the deadlock. Jefferson won by taking ten states to Burr's four. The Twelfth Amendment, ratified in 1804, prevented this from happening again by requiring a separate vote for the president and vice president.*

㉖ *The years were 1936 and 1965. In the election of 1936 Democrats Franklin Delano Roosevelt and John Nance Garner were nominated by acclamation with fifty-six seconding speeches. Lyndon Johnson and Hubert Humphrey were nominated in 1965 without a delegate vote.*

㉗ *Congressman James Garfield. None of the three most popular candidates—Ulysses S. Grant, supported by some for a third term, James G. Blaine, and Treasury Secretary John Sherman—could muster a majority vote. Thirty-six ballots later, Garfield was nominated as a compromise candidate, though he did not want the job. When he protested, he was ruled out of order, and the voting continued, making him the party's nominee.*

㉘ *(a) The Chicago Seven, (b) Bobby Seale was granted a separate trial.*

㉙ *President Herbert Hoover made those lofty promises during the 1928 presidential campaign.*

㉚ *Miriam "Ma" Ferguson of Texas and Nellie Taylor Ross of Wyoming. Ferguson's husband, the former Texas governor, was impeached in 1917 after being charged with using state moneys for his personal use. She supposedly ran to clear his name. Ross was elected to finish out her late husband's gubernatorial term.*

㉛ *(a) .2%. The vote was so close that Nixon did not concede the election until one PM the next day.*

㉜ *1836. Richard Mentor Johnson, vice president to Martin Van Buren. No candidate had received a majority of electoral votes.*

㉝ *Senator Thomas Eagleton. He was forced to withdraw two and one-half weeks later and R. Sargent Shriver (John F. Kennedy's brother-in-law) became George McGovern's running mate.*

㉞ *Democrat Samuel Tilden. He garnered 184 electoral votes but needed 185 for a majority. (Nineteen electoral votes from three Southern states were disputed, plus one from Oregon on a technicality.) Congress then appointed a special electoral commission which voted eight to seven, on a strict party vote, in favor of Rutherford B. Hayes.*

㉟ *Franklin Delano Roosevelt in 1944.* He also went on to win a fourth term. The Twenty-second Amendment was passed in 1951 to limit a president to two terms.

㊱ *James Madison.* The big event was staged at Long's Hotel on Capitol Hill on March 4, 1809. Over the years, the inaugural event has become a much bigger production, requiring the president to go "party-hopping" to six or seven inaugural balls located around town.

㊲ *Union general George B. McClellan* could not support the Democratic platform that called for an immediate and negotiated end to the Civil War. He believed that such a philosophy was detrimental to the country and was an insult to those who had risked their lives to save the Union. McClellan suffered a crushing defeat to Lincoln—212 electoral votes to 21.

㊳ *The election of 1848.*

㊴ *William Henry Harrison.* Until Ronald Reagan, Harrison, at the age of sixty-eight, was the oldest man to win the presidency. Standing in blustery cold March weather, he gave an hour and forty minute inaugural address, the longest in history. Shortly thereafter, he developed pneumonia and pleurisy from which he never recovered. He had the shortest term of any president.

40 *1940. The Republicans televised their convention from Philadelphia where Wendell Willkie received his party's nomination.*

41 *Richard Nixon. This was one of many tactics he used that earned him the epithet "Tricky Dick."*

42 *Senator Alan Cranston of California ran on an antinuclear weapons platform.*

43 *Frederick Douglass. The former slave and abolitionist received one vote during the 1888 Republican convention in Chicago.*

44 *Chicago, Illinois (twenty-four conventions). The second highest—Baltimore, Maryland—is far behind with ten.*

45 *(a) 1832. (b) The Democratic party held their first convention in Baltimore. Andrew Jackson was nominated, and the rule requiring a two-thirds majority vote for a nominee was implemented.*

46 *1856 in Philadelphia. John C. Fremont was the party's presidential nominee.*

47 *Harry S Truman's inauguration on January 20, 1949, was the first to be televised.*

48 *Democrat Franklin Delano Roosevelt in 1932.*

49 *Republican Thomas Dewey in 1944.*

50 *1840. The Democratic party created a brief platform calling for the strict interpretation of the Constitution, as well as opposition to a national bank and protective tariff.*

51 *(a) Lyndon B. Johnson. (b) He took the oath aboard Air Force One, returning to Washington from Dallas, Texas, just ninety-eight minutes after John F. Kennedy was declared dead. Mrs. Jacqueline Kennedy was at Johnson's side as he was sworn in. The deceased president's body was on that flight.*

52 *Both Fillmore and Ford became presidents without an election, and both failed to be elected in their own right. Fillmore was not renominated by the Whig party in 1874, and Gerald Ford lost to Jimmy Carter in the general election of 1976.*

53 *(b) $100,000. This was double the amount spent by his Democratic opponent, Stephen Douglas.*

54 *James Garfield. In the election of 1880 he spent $1,100,000 compared to his Democratic opponent, Winfield S. Hancock, who spent only $335,000.*

(55) *James Buchanan. He failed to win the Democratic nomination in the elections of 1844, 1848, and 1852, finally gaining enough exposure and popularity to defeat Whig candidate Millard Fillmore and Republican John C. Fremont in 1856.*

(56) *Walter Mondale. AFL-CIO convention delegates in Hollywood, Florida, voted to endorse him as the Democratic presidential nominee in the election of 1984.*

(57) *Ella Grasso of Connecticut. A victim of cancer, she resigned on December 31, 1980, and died about one month later.*

(58) *Edmund Brown. He was the incumbent, having served as California's governor from 1959 to 1967.*

(59) *John Charles Fremont. The former California Senator was well-known as an explorer and soldier. Running in 1856, when the party was only two years old, Fremont made a respectable showing, winning 114 electoral votes versus James Buchanan's 174.*

(60) *(a) New York Congressman William E. Miller. (b) Goldwater described the upstate New Yorker and former Republican national committee chairman as "a fast talking quipster with a biting wit," who had "driven Lyndon Johnson nuts in the past with his sharp*

tongue. We'd need a bit of such humor in the campaign to keep LBJ at bay."

(61) *Franklin Pierce. His backing of the Kansas-Nebraska Act of 1850 infuriated his antislavery supporters in the North. James Buchanan beat him and Senator Stephen Douglas for the presidential spot on the Democratic ticket in 1856.*

(62) *George Washington. He carried all ten states that were participating and all sixty-nine electoral votes during the election of 1789. In 1792 he again carried all of the electoral votes (132) during the election for his second term.*

(63) *Geraldine Ferraro. She ran for vice president on the Democratic ticket with Walter Mondale in 1984, making her the first woman to be selected by a major party for the vice presidency.*

(64) *Jesse Jackson, a forty-two-year-old Baptist minister and a disciple of the late Martin Luther King, Jr., lost his bid for the nomination in Atlanta at the 1984 Democratic convention. However, he used his strong influence with the black voters to gain concessions in the Democratic platform.*

(65) *Martin Van Buren. Running as a Democrat in the election of 1840, he was defeated by Whig candidate William Henry Har-*

rison. Van Buren ran again on the Free-Soil Party ticket in 1848, but lost to Zachary Taylor.

66 *The derogatory comment was made about George McGovern in the 1972 election.*

67 *Then Secretary of State John Quincy Adams. Plumer disliked Monroe and wanted to keep President Washington's record intact as the only president unanimously selected by the Electoral College.*

68 *Lee Iacocca. A committee to draft Iacocca for the 1988 Democratic presidential nomination was formed, but he told them he was not interested in the job.*

69 *Senator Joe Biden, Jr. In his closing remarks in an Iowa debate in 1987, he used the rhetoric of a British Labour party leader without giving attribution. He also admitted to having plagiarized while a student at Syracuse University Law School. But it was the revelation that he had made inaccurate claims regarding several college degrees and other exaggerated academic accomplishments that finally forced him to withdraw from the presidential race.*

70 *Political Action Committee. PACs are groups created by organizations, corporations, or labor unions to raise political funds for candidates.*

⑦ *1(c), 2(g), 3(f), 4(e),
5(b), 6(d), 7(h), 8(a).*

⑫ *Alexander Hamilton.
Burr challenged Hamilton to a duel in July 1804
after Hamilton's political scheming prevented Burr
from winning both the presidency in 1800 and the
governorship of New York in 1804. Hamilton was
fatally wounded and Burr's political career took a
nosedive.*

Political Parties
and Organizations

American politics *is supposedly controlled by two major political parties, yet other organizations ranging from the National Rifle Association to the American Vegetarian Party play a role in letting all viewpoints be heard and considered. It's all part of democracy. How's your knowledge of political parties and other organizations? Let's find out.*

① Theodore Roosevelt was a Republican when elected in 1904, but when he ran for the presidency again in 1912 against then-President Taft, he did so on a third party ticket. Name the party.

② This 1968 Democratic presidential candidate ran as an independent in the 1976 election without a vice presidential candidate. Who was he and why didn't he share the ticket?

3 Presidents William Henry Harrison, John Tyler, Zachary Taylor, and Millard Fillmore were neither Democrats nor Republicans. What political party did they represent?

4 Abraham Lincoln did not run as a Republican in 1864. What was the name of his party?

5 In 1920 Roger Baldwin was one of the founders of an organization created to protect the civil liberties of Americans. Name the organization.

6 A Democratic presidential candidate in the elections of 1952 and 1956 once said, "An independent is a guy who wants to take the politics out of politics." Who was he?

7 Who was the newspaperman who ran against Ulysses S. Grant on the Liberal Republican party ticket in the election of 1872, winning sixty-six electoral votes to the president's 286?

8 Name the ultraright wing, anticommunist organization formed in 1958 by candy manufacturer Robert Welch.

9 Republican congressman Fiorello H. La Guardia turned to a third party when he ran for mayor of New York City because the Republican party rejected his liberal views. What was the third party?

10 What still active political party is the oldest third party in U.S. history?

11 In 1920 Eugene Victor Debs ran as a presidential candidate for this party, winning 919,799 votes while an inmate at the Atlanta Federal Penitentiary. Name the party.

⑫ Whig candidate Zachary Taylor defeated Democratic candidate Lewis Cass in the presidential election of 1848. He also beat third party candidate and former president Martin Van Buren. On what ticket did the latter run?

⑬ Stokely Carmichael and H. Rapp Brown were leaders of what black militant group in the late 1960s?

⑭ In 1872 a woman newspaper editor and former clairvoyant ran against Ulysses S. Grant for the presidency on the Equal Rights ticket, and in 1892 she ran against Grover Cleveland on both the Women's Suffrage ticket and Humanitarian ticket. Who was she?

⑮ In the 1840s, a political party known as the American party was formed in opposition to the influx of immigrants. Because of the American party's desire to keep their meetings secret, those outside the party gave it a different name. What was it?

⑯ A former vice president ran against President Harry S Truman on the Progressive party ticket of 1948, opposing the Cold War policies of the United States. Who was he?

⑰ This civil rights organization was started in 1910 by both blacks and whites to bring about desegregation and equal rights for minorities without violence. Its most prominent co-founder was black activist W.E.B. Du Bois. Name the organization.

18 Name the president of the American Federation of Labor who said, "The labor of a human being is not a commodity or article of commerce. You can't weigh the soul of a man with a bar of pig iron"?

19 In the presidential election of 1844 James G. Birney of the Liberty Abolitionist party managed to win enough antislavery votes in New York to help push James Polk over the top. Name the Whig candidate he helped defeat by his third party candidacy.

20 A son of former president Franklin Roosevelt ran unsuccessfully for governor of New York in 1966. Unlike his father, Franklin D. Roosevelt, Jr. did not run as a Democrat. On what ticket did he run?

21 In the election of 1860 Edward Everett ran for the vice presidency on a ticket opposing Abraham Lincoln. Everett was the orator who gave the keynote speech the day President Lincoln delivered the Gettysburg Address. To what party did Everett and his running mate, John Bell of Tennessee, belong?

㉒ What was the name given to Northerners who supported the Southern cause during the Civil War?

㉓ Name the secret organization of Irish-American coal miners in eastern Pennsylvania that used terrorist tactics to gain better working conditions.

㉔ This radical black militant party, led by Huey Newton, Bobby Seale, and Eldridge Cleaver during the 1970s, advocated black rights through violence and revolution. Name it.

㉕ One of the more famous white Americans attracted to the cause of the radical black militant party referred to in the preceding question held cocktail parties to raise funds for the party. Can you name him?

㉖ In the 1850s Northern Whigs, Abolitionists, Free-Soilers, and Anti-slavery Democrats joined together to form what new party?

㉗ In 1948 the keynote speaker at this party's presidential nominating convention accused incumbent president Harry S Truman of wanting "to reduce us to the status of a mongrel, inferior race, mixed in blood, our Anglo-Saxon heritage a mockery." What was the party?

28 In the 1980 presidential election Ed Clark ran against Republican Ronald Reagan and Democrat Jimmy Carter. What party ran Clark as its candidate?

29 What segregationist ran for president in 1968 on the American Independent party ticket, receiving the most popular votes of any third party candidate in U.S. history?

30 What humorist said, "I belong to no organized political party—I am a Democrat"?

31 In 1970 a group of women joined to form a party opposing abortion, running Ellen McCormack as a presidential candidate in 1980. Name the party.

32 What party was created in 1874 by economically depressed farmers to encourage the use of paper currency?

33 White robes and burning crosses are the symbols of this anti-Semitic and racist organization. Name the group.

34 He was the first Socialist congressman, beginning his first term in 1911. Who was he?

35 What party ticket did John Quincy Adams run on in the election of 1824?

36 What is the nickname for the group within the Republican party that supported Democratic candidate Grover Cleveland in the election of 1884 instead of their own party's candidate, James Blaine?

37 Norman Thomas ran for the U.S. presidency six times. On what ticket did he run?

38 This group received the Nobel Peace Prize in 1977 for its work in the release of political prisoners throughout the world. Name it.

39 Operation Rescue was a New York based organization, active in the late 1980s, that was intent upon abolishing what practice?

40 In the election of 1980 President Jimmy Carter refused to participate in the first scheduled television debates against Ronald Reagan because a third party candidate from the National Unity party was included in the debate. Who was he?

41 Pediatrician Benjamin Spock ran on an anti-Vietnam War platform in the 1972 presidential election. What was his party?

42 Gus Hall was the Communist party's presidential candidate in the election of 1980. His running mate was a woman and she was black. Who was she?

43 This political party, running its first presidential candidate in 1832, opposed elitist and secret societies. Although it had little political influence, it was the first party to hold a national nominating convention and to adopt a national platform. What was the party?

44 In 1980 the Citizens party nominated one of the country's most outspoken environmental advocates as its presidential candidate. Who was he?

45 Early statesmen believed political parties were not necessary because they would only generate corruption and divisiveness. But in the early 1790s factions inevitably formed. One faction was led by Secretary of the Treasury Alexander Hamilton and Vice President John Adams. It supported a strong centralized government and represented the needs of the wealthy merchants, landowners, and manufacturers. Name the party.

46 The opposing faction of the party referred to in the preceding question ultimately evolved into the modern day Democratic party. What two statesmen led this faction?

47 What party was created in 1832 to oppose Andrew Jackson, supporting a national bank and high tariffs?

48 This group was founded in 1967 by Betty Friedan. It became the most influential women's rights organization in the United States. Name it.

49 The Democratic party took its name in whose administration?

50 Martin Luther King, Jr. created this organization in 1957 to advance the rights of blacks through nonviolence. For a two-parter: (a) name the organization, and (b) Dr. King's successor as the organization's leader?

51 El-Hajj Malik El-Shabazz was a black militant leader in the late 1950s and 1960s who became one of the most vocal spokesmen for the Black Muslim (Nation of Islam) faith, believing in black separatism. His militant views softened when he converted to Orthodox Islam. In 1965 he was assassinated by three men, two of whom were members of the Black Muslims. By what name is he best known?

52 Name the famous aviator who, in 1940, took a prominent role in supporting U.S. neutrality in the war in Europe as a member of the "America First Committee."

53 A well-known TV evangelist created the religious/political "Moral Majority," spending millions in campaign dollars to oppose liberal candidates running for Congress. Who was this evangelist?

54 Who was the black nationalist who championed a "back to Africa" movement for American blacks in the early 1920s?

55 The Afro-American movement has had its "black power." What is the movement of older Americans called?

56 Name the former California migrant worker whose name is synonymous with boycotts of table grapes and lettuce. For extra credit, name the organization he founded.

57 What citizens' lobbying group, created in 1970, by John Gardner, has been instrumental in bringing about governmental and election reform?

58 Here's a two-parter: (a) the "GOP" is another name for what party, and (b) what does it stand for?

59 What organization, following the credo, "Honor the dead by helping the living," lobbies for better benefits and financial help for former servicemen?

60 Two women were the driving force behind the women's suffrage movement in the 1860s, creating the National Woman's Suffrage Association. Name them.

61 What lobbying group is most active in opposing gun control legislation in Congress?

62 Anti-hood laws of the Ku Klux Klan were struck down in some Southern states in the 1920s, largely because of the activities of a "league" that fought prejudice and stereotyping of Jewish citizens. Name the organization.

63 This delegate to the United Nations said, "The Democrats are in a real bind. They won't get elected unless things get worse, and things won't get worse unless they get elected"?

64 Amazing but true: only three Republicans ever completed two full terms as president. Who were they?

65 In 1860 Abraham Lincoln became the first Republican elected president. Since then, how many Republican presidents have there been?

Answers

1 *Theodore Roosevelt ran on the Progressive, or Bull Moose, party in 1912.*

② *Eugene McCarthy.*
He believed the job of vice president should be eliminated.

③ *The Whigs. This party was created to provide opposition to Andrew Jackson and the Democratic party. It developed out of the National Republican party and a few smaller factions.*

④ *The Republican party temporarily switched its name to the Union party, trying to appeal to Democrats who favored the Union cause.*

⑤ *The American Civil Liberties Union or the ACLU.*

⑥ *Adlai Stevenson.*

⑦ *Horace Greeley, editor of* The New York Tribune. *In addition to the Liberal Republican party, he had the support of the Democrats.*

⑧ *The John Birch Society. Birch was an army intelligence officer and a Baptist missionary murdered in China by Communists ten days after the end of World War II in Asia. The John Birch Society claimed he was the first American to die as a result of the Cold War with the Communists. The organization worked for the abolition of social security, the income tax, and diplomatic relations with the Soviet Union.*

⑨ *The Fusion party. La Guardia was so popular that his party affiliation was irrelevant; he won not only the election of 1933, but also elections of 1937 and 1941. Nicknamed "The Little Flower" because of the Italian translation of his first name, he cleaned up New York City government and became nationally known and respected.*

⑩ *The Prohibitionist party. James Black was their first presidential candidate in 1872. In addition to its antialcohol stand, the party was the first to support the voting rights of women.*

⑪ *The Socialist party. Debs, an organizer of the Socialist party, ran as its candidate in five presidential elections. As a pacifist, he spoke out in 1918 against U.S. participation in World War I, and was sentenced to ten years in prison for violating the Espionage Act. Three years later he was pardoned by President Warren Harding.*

⑫ *The Free-Soil party ticket. The new party opposed the expansion of slavery into any territory the United States acquired in the Mexican War. The party won ten percent of the vote.*

⑬ *The Student Non-Violent Coordinating Committee (SNCC), pronounced "SNICK."*

⑭ *Victoria Woodhull. In 1871 she became the first woman to address the*

House Judiciary Committee when she argued that women and blacks were being denied their constitutional right to vote.

⑮ *The Know-Nothing party. When people asked party members about their meetings, they responded, "I know nothing about it."*

⑯ *Henry Wallace. He was vice president during Franklin Delano Roosevelt's third term but lost his spot on the ticket in 1944 when he was replaced by Harry Truman.*

⑰ *The National Association for the Advancement of Colored People (NAACP).*

⑱ *Samuel Gompers. The workingman's crusader for better working conditions and pay, he was the first president of the American Federation of Labor and, with the exception of one year, held the post from 1886 to his death in 1924.*

⑲ *Henry Clay. Fervent abolitionists voted for Birney because both Clay and Polk owned slaves.*

⑳ *The Liberal party. Roosevelt split the opposition with Democratic candidate Frank O'Connor, helping Nelson A. Rockefeller's reelection to a third term.*

㉑ *The Constitutional Union party. The party's only concerns were "the*

Constitution of the Country, the Union of the States, and the Enforcement of the Laws." It did well in the election of 1860, winning over twelve and a half percent of the vote.

㉒ *Copperheads. Northerners loyal to Lincoln's administration believed this Democratic splinter group, sympathetic to the Southern cause, resembled the venomous copperhead snake.*

㉓ *The Molly Maguires. Mine owners used police to break up the organization, which often threatened, and even murdered, some mine operators. Nineteen or twenty Molly Maguires were hanged.*

㉔ *The Black Panther party. The party's violent activities resulted in jail for its leaders on various charges, including manslaughter.*

㉕ *Leonard Bernstein.*

㉖ *The Republican party.*

㉗ *The "Dixiecrats" (States Rights Democratic party).*

㉘ *The Libertarian party. Clark received over 900,000 votes, running on a platform of eliminating business and farming subsidies, abolishing all governmental regulatory agencies, and reducing welfare.*

㉙ *George Wallace. His strong showing as a third party candidate drew votes from Democratic candidate Hubert Humphrey, with Republican Richard Nixon winning by only eight-tenths of one percent.*

㉚ *Will Rogers.*

㉛ *The Right-to-Life party.*

㉜ *The Greenback party. Its first presidential candidate was Peter Cooper in 1876, but he made a rather poor showing. The party died out in 1878, but its agrarian members joined forces with a group of workers to create the Greenback-Labor Party.*

㉝ *The Ku Klux Klan. The group was active in the presidential election of 1928, campaigning hard against Catholic candidate Al Smith. In the 1960s the growing strength of the civil rights movement caused the organization's resurgence.*

㉞ *Victor Louis Berger. In 1918 he won reelection but was sentenced to twenty years in prison for sedition and was ejected from Congress by the courts. He returned as a U.S. representative in 1923 when the Supreme Court reversed his conviction.*

㉟ *None. There were no party affiliations during that election. National po-*

litical conventions had not yet emerged, the congressional caucus system for nominating candidates was under attack, and regions of the country supporting a candidate became more important than party tags. It wasn't until the election of 1828 that distinct political parties emerged, with John Quincy Adams running again, this time on the National Republican ticket and Andrew Jackson running as a Democrat.

㊱ *The Mugwumps.*

㊲ *The Socialist party ticket. Thomas also ran for governor of New York and mayor of New York City.*

㊳ *Amnesty International. The organization, founded in 1961, has attracted many national figures, including Joan Baez, William F. Buckley, Jr., and Zbigniew Brzezinski, who served on its advisory council.*

㊴ *Abortion. Led by Randall Terry, the group attempted to block the entrance to abortion clinics, resulting in many arrests.*

㊵ *John B. Anderson, congressman from Illinois. In April of 1980, Anderson switched from running as a Republican candidate to an independent. Carter said he felt it unfair for a sole Democrat to be debating two Republicans at one time. He also perceived Anderson as a strong candidate, perhaps more of a threat than Reagan.*

(41) *The People's party.*

(42) *Angela Davis. A black activist, Davis was a controversial professor at UCLA. She was charged and then tried for helping in a courtroom escape attempt that ended in the death of four people. She was acquitted.*

(43) *The Anti-Masonic party. Its candidate, William Wirt, won only seven electoral votes in the election of 1832 against Democratic candidate Andrew Jackson and National Republican candidate Henry Clay.*

(44) *Barry Commoner, a professor, biologist, and author of several environmental books.*

(45) *The Federalist party.*

(46) *Thomas Jefferson and James Madison led the Anti-Federalist party.*

(47) *The National Republican party. Their presidential candidate was Henry Clay. Making a poor showing in the election of 1832, the party merged with other factions to create the Whig party by 1836.*

(48) *The National Organization For Women (NOW). The organization worked for the passage of the Equal Rights Amendment and for equal footing with men in the work force, government, and in all facets of life.*

(49) *Andrew Jackson. He served as president from 1829 to 1837.*

(50) *(a) The Southern Christian Leadership Conference (SCLC). (b) Ralph David Abernathy became the organization's leader after King was assassinated in 1968.*

(51) *Malcolm X.*

(52) *Charles Lindbergh. The "America First Committee" was one of the most outspoken groups advocating isolationism. His father had been a Minnesota congressman.*

(53) *Jerry Falwell. His Moral Majority organization was opposed to homosexuals, abortion, and the Equal Rights Amendment, but favored school prayer and the teaching of creationism. He took over control of the PTL (Praise the Lord) Club when its leader, Jim Bakker, stepped down after his extramarital affair was revealed, later to be convicted of fraud and conspiracy.*

(54) *Marcus Garvey. The native Jamaican pushed for a bill of rights for blacks, an annual national black holiday on August 31, and a steamship line to transport blacks back to Africa. His goals were never realized because he was convicted of mail fraud in 1925 in connection with mishandling funds to be used for the steamship company. After serving time in prison, he was deported to Jamaica in 1927.*

(55) *Gray Power.*

(56) *Cesar Chavez. As founder and president of the National Farm Workers Association in 1962, which later became the United Farm Workers in 1972, he used boycotts and strikes against grape and lettuce growers to gain union contracts for the workers.*

(57) *Common Cause. The organization has been credited with bringing about more stringent campaign disclosure requirements, voting rights for eighteen- year-olds, and the congressional approval of the Equal Rights Amendment. Gardner was President Lyndon Johnson's secretary of housing and urban development from 1965 to 1969 before creating the organization.*

(58) *The Republican Party. "GOP" stands for Grand Old Party.*

(59) *Veterans of Foreign Wars of the United States (VFW). The group, often associated with the red crepe paper poppy flower sold to raise money for former servicemen, has been a strong lobbying group for governmental assistance and benefits on Capitol Hill.*

(60) *Susan B. Anthony and Elizabeth Stanton Cady. Believing women were entitled to the same franchise rights granted to freedmen through the Fifteenth Amendment, they created*

the National Woman's Suffrage Association (NWSA), to lobby Congress and gain public support.

⑥ *The National Rifle Association (NRA) is a strong opponent of gun control legislation.*

⑥ *The organization is the Anti-Defamation League, a program of B'nai B'rith, which was founded in 1913.*

⑥ *Jeane Kirkpatrick. In 1981 President Reagan appointed her as a permanent United States representative to the United Nations.*

⑥ *Ulysses S. Grant, Dwight Eisenhower, and Ronald Reagan.*

⑥ *Seventeen Republicans and eight Democrats.*

Events and Issues

This chapter is *going to test your knowledge of the political events and issues that have shaped our history. It obviously doesn't attempt to include all of them, but we've tried to touch on the more important and memorable.*

❶ In the early 1960s the women's liberation movement received a major push from Betty Friedan, a social reformer and psychologist, when she published a book contending that housewives were bored and needed to develop their own feelings of self-worth. Name the book.

❷ What was the name of the black leader and national chairman of the Student Non-Violent Coordinating Committee (SNCC) who made "Black Power" a popular phrase in the mid-1960s?

3 What system, used to achieve equality in minority hiring, was discontinued in 1984 by the Commission on Civil Rights?

4 Try this three-parter: (a) which U.S. representative introduced the Equal Rights Amendment, (b) what organization fought particularly hard for its passage, and (c) what famous homemaker battled vigorously for its defeat?

5 In the late 1980s the country found itself embroiled in the issue of surrogate motherhood. "Baby M" was the center of the national controversy after William and Elizabeth Stern contracted with a surrogate mother to be artificially inseminated and to carry the baby to full term for them. After the baby's birth, the surrogate mother changed her mind, claiming that "Baby M" was rightfully hers. Who was the surrogate mother?

6 Name the woman from Oklahoma whose death in a suspicious auto accident brought the danger of nuclear power to the attention of Capitol Hill and the American people. (Hint: Meryl Streep portrayed her in a movie.)

7 The question of how far citizens may go in physically protecting themselves became a political "hot potato" in the 1980s. Who was nicknamed the "Subway Vigilante" when he shot teenagers he believed were attempting to rob him on a New York subway?

8 What endangered species owes its continued existence to the United States Supreme Court for halting the completion of the Tellico Dam in Tennessee in 1978?

9 Name the radical political group, created in 1960 in New York by Tom Hayden and Al Haber, that opposed discrimination and militarism.

10 Can you name the world heavyweight champion boxer who was stripped of his title and faced criminal charges in 1967 for avoiding the draft?

11 What famous black contralto was to perform at Constitution Hall in April 1939 but was denied that opportunity by the owners of the Hall, the Daughters of the American Revolution?

12 Name the black woman who, in December 1955, in Montgomery, Alabama, refused to give her bus seat to a white passenger, resulting in her arrest and a city-wide boycott by blacks.

13 In 1954 two words were added to the United States Pledge of Allegiance. What were they?

14 From 1980 to January 1981 American hostages were held by Iran. For a two-parter: (a) how many Americans were held, and (b) how many days were they held?

15 What NAACP leader, known as "Mississippi's Martin Luther King," was shot to death in Jackson, Mississippi in June 1963?

16 Sirhan Sirhan, a Jordanian immigrant, assassinated Senator Robert Kennedy on June 6, 1968, just two months after Martin Luther King was murdered. Sirhan's act was politically motivated. Why did he shoot Kennedy, who was then a presidential candidate?

17 In 1963 what governor stood in the "schoolhouse door" of a southern university attempting to block the entrance of two black students?

18 The leaders of the United States, Egypt, and Israel signed an historic peace treaty on March 26, 1979. Who were the three leaders? For extra credit, what was the popular name for this peace treaty?

19 What group was responsible for bombing the U.S. Capitol in 1971 as a protest against the United States military involvement in Indochina?

20 Name the 1968 incident that resulted in the massacre by American soldiers of hundreds of innocent Vietnamese—old men, women, and children—during the Vietnam War.

㉑ When the fatal shot struck Martin Luther King, Jr. in 1968, he was talking to another civil rights activist at his motel as he leaned over a second story balcony. For a three-parter: (a) with whom was he talking, (b) in what city did the assassination take place, and (c) why was King there?

㉒ The safety of nuclear power became the focus of many demonstrations in the late 1970s and 1980s. The worst nuclear accident in United States history occurred in 1979 at what plant in Pennsylvania?

㉓ In 1987 a U.S. Navy frigate was accidentally attacked in the Persian Gulf by an Iraqi war plane, and thirty-seven American sailors were killed. Name the vessel.

㉔ In April 1970 President Nixon sent American and South Vietnamese troops into what country, even though, according to pollsters, forty-eight percent of Americans disapproved?

㉕ In May 1970 fifteen university students were gunned down by National

Guardsmen during an anti-war rally that had been prohibited by the governor. At what university did this tragedy occur?

26 A South Korean Boeing 747 airliner was shot down by a Soviet fighter plane as the aircraft strayed into air space over Soviet bases in September 1983. Sixty-one Americans were among the 269 killed, including the leader of the extremely conservative John Birch Society. Who was he?

27 In 1968 an American ship was captured by North Korean patrol boats. Name the vessel and, for extra credit, the American captain who came close to being court-martialed over the incident.

28 On May 4, 1886, a labor strike in Chicago turned into a riot when a bomb exploded killing eleven people and injuring over one hundred. Name the riot.

29 Who was the first black student to enter the University of Mississippi?

30 In 1961 an unsuccessful attempt by the United States to help overthrow the Cuban regime of Fidel Castro failed miserably. What was this incident called?

31 In November 1978 the

former city supervisor of San Francisco shot the city's mayor and the new supervisor. For this three-parter, name (a) the assassin, (b) the mayor, and (c) the new supervisor.

32 During the 1900s a group of socially conscious American writers used their literary talents to reveal corruption in American politics and society. (a) What derogatory name did President Teddy Roosevelt give these writers, and (b) can you name three of the writers?

33 In 1953 an American husband and wife were executed for selling classified information to the Soviet Union. Who were they?

34 Beginning in 1980, thousands of Cubans, many of them criminals or mentally ill, arrived in the United States. What was the name of the boatlift?

35 In 1961 civil rights activists rode on buses throughout the South, testing the acceptance of federally mandated desegregation. What was their action called?

36 Politics reach every part of life—even the arts. Two male Soviet ballet dancers defected to the United States, one in 1970, the other in 1974. Who were they?

37 Fearful of a Soviet-

Cuban military buildup, the United States invaded and occupied a Caribbean nation in 1983, rescuing several hundred American medical students who were trapped there after a military coup. Name the country.

38 Congress designated April 22, 1970, as a special day of awareness for the country. (a) What was the event called, and (b) what "cause" was the focus?

39 In January 1969 hijackings of U.S. airplanes became epidemic. What was the destination of the hijackers at that time?

40 Marcus Wayne Chenault testified in court that God had commanded him to kill the father of a deceased civil rights crusader. Instead, he chose an easier target, the leader's mother. Whom did he kill?

41 Name the ghetto neighborhood in Los Angeles that was the scene of five days of racial violence and rioting in the mid-1960s.

42 After a lengthy investigation, what panel concluded that the president's Secret Service protection needed to be improved, and that the murder of a president or vice president should be a federal offense?

43 In June 1982, over fifteen hundred protestors were arrested in New York City as they surrounded the United Nations embassies of the United States, France, China, England and Russia. What were they protesting?

44 In 1963 a type of communication was set up between the United States and the Soviet Union to avoid any chance of either power deploying nuclear weapons by mistake. What was this communication called?

45 The year 1969 was eventful for world political leaders. Answer the following five questions about that year: (a) what U.S. president was inaugurated, (b) what Israeli prime minister took office, (c) what president of France resigned, (d) what former U.S. president died, and (e) what was the name of the president of North Vietnam who died?

46 In 1963 an FBI investigation concluded that the assassination of John F. Kennedy had been carried out by only one man. Here's a three-parter: (a) who was he, (b) what was the date of the assassination, and (c) from what building did the assassin shoot the president?

47 In what city did lunch counters first become integrated in 1960?

48 In 1797 President John Adams sent three representatives to negotiate peace with French foreign minister Charles Maurice de Talleyrand. They were met by three French agents who demanded a $250,000 bribe before negotiations could begin. Name the incident.

49 In March 1965 a group of civil rights activists began their historic freedom walk from Selma, Alabama, to the state's capital, Montgomery. Who led the march?

50 An American reconnaissance aircraft was gunned down over central Russia in May 1960. Give the popular name of the incident. (Hint: It was named after the type of aircraft.)

51 Here's a follow-up question: Name the pilot of the aircraft in the above-mentioned incident.

52 Known as the "Great Grain Robbery," President Nixon infuriated farmers when he negotiated a secret deal to sell American wheat at a bargain price to a foreign country in 1972. What country bought the wheat?

53 What event and date did Franklin D. Roosevelt claim would "live in infamy"?

54 Two hundred protestors occupied a Sioux Indian reservation for sixty-nine days in 1973, demanding a Senate investigation into charges of civil rights violations. Where was the Indian reservation, and why was that site selected?

55 What nineteenth-century New Yorker can take credit for having 3,000 obscenity violators arrested and for destroying 160 tons of art and literature?

56 Americans sat in line for hours at gas pumps paying exorbitant prices after the oil embargo of 1973. Why did the Arab countries cut off the oil to the United States?

57 On July 23, 1967, the nation experienced its worst race riots in history. Name the city where they took place.

58 A United States congressman was murdered in Jonestown, Guyana, in 1978 when he investigated reports that the leader of the People's Temple was mistreating cult members and was threatening to order a mass suicide. For a two-parter: name (a) the congressman and (b) the cult leader.

59 In 1962 President Kennedy discovered that the Soviet Union had been secretly constructing missile installations on an island in the West Indies. What's the popular name of this "crisis"?

60 Senator Edward Kennedy praised President Carter for an action he took only one day after his inauguration, calling it "a major, impressive, and compassionate step towards healing the wounds of Vietnam." What did Carter do to receive such accolades?

61 The famine and suffering in this republic, formerly known as East Pakistan, caught the attention of the world in the early 1970s. Name the country.

62 The United States dropped atomic bombs on two Japanese cities in August 1945, ending World War II. Name those two cities.

63 Court-ordered busing in this Northern city led to violence and gang wars in the fall of 1974. What was the city?

64 In 1972 the United States and the Soviet Union held talks that produced a treaty limiting antiballistic missiles and offensive nuclear weapons. What were the talks called?

65 This educator was the first black to be invited, and to accept, a dinner invitation to the White House. Who was he?

66 Louisa Swain goes down in history for what important event: (a) the first woman in the United States to vote legally, (b) the first woman to be elected to the U.S. Senate, or (c) the first woman to test the abortion issue in the U.S. Supreme Court, the actual plaintiff in *Roe v. Wade?*

67 During the late nineteenth century, a temperance zealot put terror in the hearts and minds of Midwest saloon owners as she went from town to town with a hatchet, destroying property and bottles of booze. Her one-woman campaign helped pave the way for Prohibition and the Eighteenth Amendment. Who was she?

68 In 1978 the U.S. Postal Service issued the first postage stamp in honor of a black woman. Who was she?

69 Name the wealthy Dallas oil baron, who, despite his support of John F. Kennedy in the election of 1960, later received criticism from the president for using IRS loopholes to avoid paying his fair share of federal income taxes.

Answers

1 The Feminine Mystique. *The book, published in 1963, encouraged thousands of women to take up the cause of women's rights.*

2 *Stokely Carmichael. He left SNCC in 1967 to become the prime minister of* *the more militant Black Panther party. However, when that group embraced white radicals, he resigned and left the black movement, exiling himself to Guinea.*

③ *The quota system. The Equal Employment Opportunity Commission created hiring quotas in the 1960s to end racial discrimination.*

④ *(a) Representative Martha Griffith, Democrat from Michigan, (b) National Organization for Women, and (c) Phyllis Schlafly.*

⑤ *(5) Mary Beth Whitehead. A nasty legal battle ensued but was resolved in 1988 when the court determined that the Sterns should have custody of the baby but that Whitehead should have liberal visitation privileges.*

⑥ *Karen Silkwood. As an employee at a nuclear power facility that processed nuclear fuel rods, she claimed she had been contaminated by plutonium. En route to discussing her fears with a reporter, she was killed in an automobile accident. Silkwood's battle went on even after her death, with her heirs receiving an out-of-court settlement of $1.38 million from the Kerr-McGee Plant.*

⑦ *Bernard Goetz. He was found not guilty of attempted murder, but was sentenced to one year in prison for illegal gun possession.*

⑧ *The snail darter. The Tennessee Valley Authority convinced the court that the designated Tellico Dam area was the only known habitat of the three-inch fresh water fish.*

⑨ *Students for a Demo-cratic Society (SDS). The group was most active in the late sixties.*

⑩ *Cassius Clay (Muham-mad Ali). He claimed he should be exempt because he was a Black Muslim minister, and joining the military would violate his religious beliefs. A Texas court sentenced him to five years and fined him $10,000, but in June 1971 the U.S. Supreme Court overturned the conviction.*

⑪ *Marian Anderson. First Lady Eleanor Roosevelt then resigned from the Daughters of the American Revolution and arranged for another recital for the singer before a crowd of 75,000 at the Lincoln Memorial on April 9, 1939.*

⑫ *Rosa Parks. The boycott lasted for a year, ending only when the city an-nounced it would comply with the November 13, 1966, Supreme Court ruling that bus segregation is unconstitutional.*

⑬ *"Under God." The phrase "one nation indivisible" was changed to "one nation, under God, indivisible. . . ." The change was instituted by a congressional resolution, signed by President Dwight Eisenhower, and, in the opinion of some, crossed over the boundaries of separation of Church and State.*

(14) *(a) 52 hostages, (b) 444 days of captivity. In April 1980 a rescue attempt orchestrated by President Jimmy Carter became a disaster, ending in eight U.S. military deaths and several injuries. The hostages were eventually freed just minutes after President Ronald Reagan was sworn in on January 21, 1981. President Carter was understandably disappointed that the release could not be achieved during his administration.*

(15) *Medgar Evers. A white man from Mississippi was unsuccessfully tried twice for the assassination, but each trial ended in a hung jury.*

(16) *Senator Robert Kennedy was considered pro-Israel, while Sirhan Sirhan, an Arab, was vehemently against Israel.*

(17) *George Wallace. He was unsuccessful, as National Guardsmen escorted the students, Vivian Malone and James Hood, into the school for registration.*

(18) *President Jimmy Carter of the United States, President Anwar el Sadat of Egypt, and Prime Minister Menachem Begin of*

Israel. In April 1979 Sadat and Begin signed the Camp David Accord.

(19) *The Weather Underground, a radical "New Left" group.*

(20) *The My Lai massacre. The incident was kept under wraps for over a year before it was finally disclosed by the U.S. Defense Department in 1969 following a veteran's letter to President Nixon. The leader of the Task Force, wrongfully believing that every resident in My Lai was either a Viet Cong or Viet Cong supporter, ordered the town destroyed.*

(21) *(a) Jesse Jackson, (b) Memphis, Tennessee, (c) Martin Luther King was there in support of a sanitation workers' strike.*

(22) *Three-Mile Island. Although no lives were lost, the accident set off a series of antinuclear demonstrations and added to the long-standing controversy over the safety of nuclear energy.*

(23) *The USS* Stark. *Iraq claimed they thought the ship was Iranian and agreed to pay $27.3 million to the families of the crew members killed in the incident.*

(24) *Cambodia. Nixon believed that the "incursion" was necessary to eliminate enemy "sanctuaries" and to facilitate eventually turning the war over to the South Vietnamese.*

㉕ *Kent State University in Kent, Ohio. Four students were killed and eleven wounded, three critically.*

㉖ *U.S. Representative Larry P. McDonald from Georgia.*

㉗ *The ship is the* Pueblo; *the ship's captain, Commander Lloyd Bucher. The eighty-two-member crew was held prisoner for almost a year. Bucher came close to being court-martialed for freely surrendering the vessel in January, 1968, and for signing an admission that the vessel was seized in North Korean waters and was on an intelligence mission.*

㉘ *The Haymarket Square Riot. Eight anarchists were put on trial for the bombing. All were convicted for inciting violence. Four were hung, one committed suicide, and three were imprisoned for seven years before being pardoned.*

㉙ *James Meredith. Demonstrators became violent, trying to block the twenty-nine-year old former Air Force sergeant's registration at the university. Federal troops were called in to quash the unrest. Two people were slain and twenty-eight marshals were wounded. Meredith graduated in 1963, despite efforts by Mississippi governor Ross Barrett to prevent him from receiving a degree.*

㉚ *The Bay of Pigs. Most of the 1,500 Cuban exiles who attempted to over-*

throw Castro in the Bay of Pigs invasion were either killed or captured. The soldiers were trained by the CIA and had the support of the U.S. government. The Cuban military had little trouble putting down the insurgence that resulted in diplomatic tension between Soviet leader Nikita Khrushchev and U.S. President John Kennedy.

③① *(a) Dan White, (b) Mayor George Moscone, and (c) Supervisor Harvey Milk. White had quit his job a few weeks earlier, but then decided he had made a mistake. He asked Mayor Moscone to give him back his job, but Moscone refused. Milk, who took White's job, was a self-proclaimed homosexual and gay activist, something White found repugnant.*

③② *(a) The Muckrakers, (b) Upton Sinclair, Lincoln Steffens, and Ida Tarbell.*

③③ *Julius and Ethel Rosenberg. Charged and convicted of espionage in 1951, they were the first civilians sentenced to death under the General Espionage Act of 1917, for turning over secret atomic information to the Soviets. The death sentences were questioned by Rosenberg supporters because the United States was not at war with the Soviets at the time of the alleged spy activities. Protestors came out in large numbers on the day of the execution, still believing it was all part of Senator Joseph McCarthy's "red scare."*

③④ *Mariel, named after a Cuban port. In 1987, when President Ronald Reagan announced a plan to send prisoners back to Cuba, riots broke out in Oakdale, Louisiana, and Atlanta, Georgia.*

③⑤ *The Freedom Riders. The civil rights activists, both white and black, were greeted with harassment and discrimination, requiring the mobilization of the National Guard in some cities.*

③⑥ *Rudolph Nureyev in 1970, and Mikhail Baryshnikov in 1974.*

③⑦ *Grenada. The United Nations passed a resolution deploring the U.S. action.*

③⑧ *(a) Earth Day; (b) the annual event calls attention to the care and preservation of the environment.*

③⑨ *Cuba. The number of planes hijacked reached forty in 1969.*

④⓪ *Mrs. Martin Luther King, Sr. The assassination took place in 1974 in the Ebenezer Baptist Church in Atlanta.*

④① *Watts. President Johnson called in the National Guard to restore order.*

④② *The Warren Commission, following the assassination of President John F. Kennedy.*

㊸ *Nuclear weapons. The five countries were chosen as targets of the massive protest because they had the capacity to wage a nuclear war.*

㊹ *The hot line. In 1962 delayed communications had been a problem during the Cuban missile crisis. The hot line was created to correct that problem.*

㊺ *(a) Richard Nixon, (b) Golda Meir, (c) Charles DeGaulle, (d) Dwight Eisenhower, and (e) Ho Chi Minh.*

㊻ *(a) Lee Harvey Oswald, (b) November 22, 1963, and (c) the Texas Book Depository building.*

㊼ *(a) San Antonio, Texas. The movement to integrate lunch counters began in February 1960 at a Woolworth's store in Charlotte, North Carolina. Black students sat down to eat, in protest of the policy that blacks had to be standing to be waited on. By the end of February, blacks in fifteen cities conducted similar protests, finally bringing about integration in San Antonio on March 21 of that year.*

㊽ *The XYZ Affair. Adams was so incensed that he ended the peace overture. When the president reported the incident to Congress, he substituted the letters X, Y, Z for the actual names of the French agents.*

(49) *Reverend Martin Luther King, Jr. Alabama Governor George Wallace was ordered by a federal court judge to refrain from interfering with the freedom walk.*

(50) *The U-2 incident. The incident caused diplomatic tension between President Eisenhower and Soviet leader Nikita Khrushchev, causing the latter to drop out of the Big Four summit conference in Paris between the U.S., the Soviet Union, England, and France.*

(51) *Francis Gary Powers. The Soviet Union convicted him of spying and sentenced him on August 17, 1960, to ten years in prison and to a work farm. One and a half years later he was traded to the United States in return for a Russian spy.*

(52) *The Soviet Union.*

(53) *The Japanese attack on Pearl Harbor on December 7, 1941. When drafting this speech to Congress, he first wrote "Yesterday, December 7, 1941, a date that will live in world history. . ." By replacing the words "world history" with "infamy," he turned a predictable phrase into one of the most often quoted in history.*

(54) *Wounded Knee, South Dakota. This was the same site as the last major battle of the Indian Wars, which took place in 1890. About 300 arrests were made during the 1973 oc-*

cupation, but the federal government agreed to investigate the allegations.

⑭ *Anthony Comstock. He dedicated his life to censorship, pushing for legislation that ultimately prohibited obscene materials from the U.S. mail system.*

⑮ *The United States supported Israel during the Yom Kippur War. The embargo lasted for about five months and was lifted on March 18, 1974.*

⑯ *Detroit, Michigan. Forty-three people were killed. Just eleven days earlier, twenty-six died in riot-torn Newark, New Jersey.*

⑰ *(a) Congressman Leo Ryan, and (b) Reverend Jim Jones. Jones shot and killed Ryan, three journalists, and two defecting cult members. Jones then ordered members to swallow poison, some drinking cyanide laced Kool-Aid. Jones ended his own life with a gun.*

⑱ *The Cuban Missile Crisis. President Kennedy responded by ordering a naval blockade on the island of Cuba. After several days of talks between the two countries, the Soviets dismantled and withdrew the weapons.*

⑲ *President Carter pardoned Vietnam draft dodgers, an act that angered some Americans.*

(61) *Bangladesh. Fund-raising campaigns were conducted for the civil war torn country with U.S. rock musicians, including Ringo Starr and Bob Dylan, performing benefit concerts.*

(62) *Hiroshima and Nagasaki were destroyed by the atomic bomb in 1945.*

(63) *Boston. The turmoil continued for several months. Students boycotted classes and fights broke out among blacks and whites. Police were sent in on October 15 after seven students were injured in the fighting.*

(64) *Strategic Arms Limitation Talks (SALT). They were followed by SALT II negotiations in 1974, then START (Strategic Arms Reduction Talks) in 1982.*

(65) *Booker T. Washington. President Teddy Roosevelt extended the invitation after being in office less than a month, a gesture not received well by Southerners.*

(66) *(a) Swain was the first woman to vote legally, the right being granted through Wyoming legislation. Women's voting rights nationally were not granted until 1920 by the nineteenth Amendment.*

(67) *Carry Nation. Her destructive activities caused her to be arrested thirty times.*

⑥⑧ *Harriet Tubman. An escaped slave, in the mid-1800s abolitionist Tubman helped more than 300 slaves gain their freedom through the Underground Railroad.*

⑥⑨ *H. L. (Haroldson Lafayette) Hunt. It was estimated that he amassed a net worth between two and three billion dollars. He used radio, television, and a newspaper column to express his strong anticommunist views. He authored a novel,* Alpaca, *about a mythical utopian country in which each citizen was given voting power based upon the amount of taxes he paid.*

The Media

Nineteenth-century writer Oscar Wilde appreciated the power of the press when he said, "In America, the President rules for four years and journalism governs for ever and ever."

The press has always had the power to change history, taking on the aristocratic label of the "fourth estate." And that influence has only increased with the advent of radio and television, and the immediacy of videotape.

Here are some questions that will test your knowledge of radio and television journalists and programs, and newspaper and magazine articles, as well as the movies and books that have played a part in U.S. politics.

❶ Which president held the first live televised news conference? For extra points, what was the year?

❷ Which president was the first to hold a news conference that was taped and aired later on television?

❸ Who was the first president to speak on television?

❹ The hot political issue of ethnic and racial prejudice was introduced into a situation comedy in 1971. Name the show.

❺ In the 1960s a vice presidential candidate was the target of a simplistic yet effective TV commercial that opened with the words "_____ for Vice President" splashed across the screen, with a man's laughter in the background. The laughter gradually faded and an announcer bluntly said, "This would be funny if it weren't so serious." Who was the vice presidential candidate?

❻ News broadcasters are expected to report the news impartially, stifling their own personal views. However, in 1968 one well-known anchor blatantly came out in opposition to the Vietnam war on national television after he traveled there and viewed it firsthand. Who was he?

7 Beginning on January 23, 1977, over half of America's TV sets were tuned into an eight-part journey through seven generations of a black family. Name the show and the author.

8 Name the outspoken Detroit priest who used his own radio show to pontificate against Jews and Franklin Delano Roosevelt, whom he labeled as "anti-God."

9 Here's a "Name Him" question. Name the newspaper editor best known for his "Go West, young man, go West" editorial advice. He was a presidential candidate in 1872, but was trounced by President Ulysses S. Grant.

10 What twentieth-century president, later dubbed the "Abdominal Showman," lifted his shirt to show reporters his scar after recent surgery.

11 In 1976 President Jimmy Carter made the mistake of telling a writer that he had often "lusted in his heart." Given the chance, Carter would probably have taken back those words in view of the controversy that arose over them. For a two-parter: (a) in what magazine did his comments appear, and (b) who was the writer?

12 Richard Nixon felt the

need for a press room in the White House. To make space for the news media, what did he have removed?

13 Who was the Kansas City news anchor who sued Metromedia for sex discrimination when she was demoted to reporter in 1983?

14 In the 1976 presidential campaign President Ford made a major factual blunder during a televised debate with Democratic candidate Jimmy Carter. He stated that there was no Soviet domination in what portion of the world?

15 Ronald Reagan was the country's only actor-turned-president. In addition to his roles in films such as *Hellcats of the Navy*, *King's Row*, and *Brother Rat and a Baby*, he hosted a Western TV series for three years, as well as an anthology series sponsored by a major utility company. Name the two programs.

16 The first televised presidential debates were held in 1960 between Richard Nixon and John F. Kennedy. For a two-parter: (a) when were the first vice presidential debates held, and (b) between what candidates?

17 The results of public opinion polls can sway voters for or against a candidate or issue. Whose name is synonymous with American opinion polls?

18 Who was the editor who published a newspaper in 1831 called *The Liberator*, which demanded the immediate freedom for all the country's slaves?

19 Name the president who selected an ordained Baptist minister to serve as his press secretary. For extra points, name the press secretary.

20 What American novelist and playwright, who ran in 1960 for a Democratic seat in Congress in upstate New York, made a spectacular showing but nevertheless lost? (Hint: His literary works include *Myra Breckenridge*, *Burr*, and *Lincoln*.)

21 Which First Lady was the first to have her own regular press conferences?

22 A retired U.S. general filed a libel suit against CBS for running the documentary "The Uncounted Enemy: A Vietnam Deception," which implied he had intentionally deceived the American people and the government about the number of North Vietnamese troops. For this two-parter: (a) who was the general, and (b) who was the reporter for CBS?

23 In 1987 the FCC dropped a thirty-eight-year-old policy requiring broadcasters to present all sides of a controversial issue. Can you (a) name the policy, and (b) explain why it was dropped?

24 In 1971 Richard Nixon had an enemies list that included Leonard Woodcock of the United Auto Workers and actor Paul Newman, considered a radical by Nixon. Who was the CBS reporter on that list?

25 Name the presidential candidate whose media campaign included a television commercial that received such a negative reaction from the American public that it ran only once.

26 This well-known writer ran for the Democratic mayoral nomination in New York City in 1969, advocating statehood for the city. His campaign slogan was "No more bullshit." Who was he?

27 Follow-up question: What controversial columnist was his running mate, seeking the presidency of New York's city council?

28 This author won a Pulitzer Prize for a novel based on the political career of Louisiana Governor Huey Long. Name the author and novel.

29 CBS canceled this

show in 1969 because its two male stars injected their political views, including anti-Vietnam War sentiments, into their comedy skits. Name the show.

30 Follow-up question: What folksinger had one of his songs, "Waist Deep in the Big Muddy," removed from the above-mentioned TV show because the network felt it was an insult to President Lyndon B. Johnson and his Vietnam policy?

31 Name the president who was forced to remain submerged in the Potomac River while a newswoman held his clothes hostage until he responded to her questions.

32 A Senate committee investigation of quiz shows ended in the conviction of English professor Charles Van Doren and several other contestants who had been given the answers prior to the show, netting them thousands of dollars in winnings. What was the name of the television show on which Van Doren appeared?

33 Who was the first president to hold regular White House news conferences?

34 Name the author who won a Pulitzer Prize for *The Making of the President, 1960*.

35 What two *Washington Post* reporters exposed the Watergate scandal in a book they co-authored, published in 1976?

36 Here's a follow-up question: A movie was released that same year about the journalists' investigative report of President Nixon's downfall. For a two-parter: (a) what was the movie, and (b) who were the actors who portrayed the journalists?

37 What famous actor, director, and filmmaker went into exile in Switzerland in 1952 after his controversial politics caused him trouble with the U.S. government?

38 What media event provided American voters with such phrases as, "There you go again," and "Are you better off than you were four years ago"? For extra points: who made these remarks?

39 In the case of *The New York Times Co. v. Sullivan*, the Court determined that a government official has to prove one element in order to be successful in a libel suit. What is that one element: (a) actual malice, (b) damages, or (c) truthfulness?

40 *The New York Evening Post* was a Federalist newspaper published in 1801. Its two publishers were prominent leaders of the time, one a former secretary of the treasury, and the other a former Supreme Court justice. Name them.

41 Which president held the first televised cabinet meeting?

42 Three presidents were formerly newspapermen. Who were they?

43 Who was the first president to hire a speech writer?

44 What news service jumped the gun in 1918 by announcing the end of World War I four days before it actually occurred?

45 Which president's campaign manager resigned because he was being investigated on cocaine charges? For extra credit, name the campaign manager.

46 This president said, "Whenever the press quits abusing me, I know I'm in the wrong pew." Who was he?

47 Which president was known for giving televised fireside chats while wearing a cardigan sweater?

48 Which TV network was the first to cover a presidential election? For extra credit, during which election?

49 *The Chicago Tribune* made a major blunder when it proclaimed Thomas Dewey the victor in a presidential election. (a) Who was the real winner, and (b) what year was the election?

50 During which presidential election were the first spot television commercials shown?

51 Vice President Richard Nixon and Soviet Premier Nikita Khrushchev held an impromptu televised debate in 1959 in Moscow. The setting of the discussion was unique. Where did it take place?

52 In the early 1980s a former Israeli defense minister sued *Time* magazine for publishing an article stating that he had encouraged the murder of Palestinians. Who was the plaintiff, and what was the jury's decision?

53 This political cartoonist received a Pulitzer Prize in 1975 for his syndicated comicstrip, Doonesbury. Name him.

54 Who was the famous radio and television announcer who introduced the president of the United States by saying, "Ladies and Gentlemen, the President of the United States, Hoobert Heever"?

55 Although this journalist is best known for his "On the Road" travelogues, he has a long history of political reporting, cohosting "CBS News Sunday Morning" and "Eyewitness to History." Who is he?

56 This news and political commentary program, bearing the name of the two cohosts, began in 1983 on the Public Broadcasting System (PBS). Name the program and full names of its hosts.

57 What author and *New York Times* columnist served as speechwriter and special assistant to President Nixon?

58 Who was the major network correspondent who was punched in the face by a security guard during rioting at the Democratic National Convention in 1968?

59 Who was the former reporter, columnist, and television commentator who is best known for her debates against James C. Kilpatrick on CBS's "60 Minutes" in the late 1970s: (a) Shana Alexander, (b) Jessica Savitch, or (c) Barbara Walters?

60 This *New York Times* political columnist won a Pulitzer prize in 1979 and has written several books including *Growing Up* and *Our Next President*. Is he (a) Tom Wicker, (b) Russell Baker, or (c) William Rukeyser.

61 Journalist Eric Sevareid said this about one of his colleagues upon his death: "He was a shooting star. We shall live in his afterglow—a very long time—we shall not see his likes again." Who was this newsman? (Hint: He produced the program "See it Now" in 1951.)

62 TV and radio journalists often make a name for themselves through the program that they host. Match the journalist with his program.

Journalist	Show
1. Ted Koppel	**(a)** "Meet the Press"
2. Dan Rather	**(b)** "NBC Nightly News"
3. John Cameron Swayze	**(c)** "Firing Line"
4. William Buckley, Jr.	**(d)** "60 Minutes"
5. Douglas Edwards	**(e)** "ABC News Nightline"
6. John Chancellor	**(f)** "Camel News Caravan"
7. Lawrence Spivak	**(g)** "Report to the Nation"
8. Edward R. Murrow	**(h)** "Person to Person"

63 Radio and television journalists are often associated with an opening or closing salutation. See how well you remember famous lines by matching the personality with his famous first or last words.

Personality	Salutation
1. Walter Winchell	**(a)** "So long until tomorrow."
2. Walter Cronkite	**(b)** "Good day!"
3. Paul Harvey	**(c)** "Thank you, Mr. President."
4. Merriman Smith	**(d)** "And that's the way it is."
5. Barbara Walters	**(e)** "We're in touch, so you be in touch."
6. Lowell Thomas	**(f)** "Mr. and Mrs. America and all the ships at sea."

64 Ralph Nader's exposé on the safety of the auto industry caused one auto maker a great deal of concern—so much that the company admitted before a congressional committee that it had hired investigators to look into the consumer advocate's politics and sexual habits. For this two-parter, name (a) the auto maker, and (b) Nader's 1965 book.

65 "The Pentagon Papers" was a top-secret study of United States involvement in Southeast Asia that revealed misconduct and deception by the U.S. government. Disillusioned with the government's stance on its presence in Vietnam, one individual leaked the study to *The New York Times* in 1971. Who was he?

66 This novelist gave the antislavery movement a shot in the arm with her popular work published in 1852. (a) Who was the author of this book, which included the villain Simon Legree, and (b) what is the title?

67 What civil rights leader was viewed in 1989 as a traitor to the Martin Luther King, Jr. camp because he wrote a book accusing King of having had an illicit sexual encounter with a woman the night he was assassinated.

68 This poet created the phrase "flower power" and was involved in protesting the Vietnam War. His best-known poem, "Howl," was written in 1956 and criticized the American way of life. Name him.

69 Name the political cartoonist responsible for popularizing the donkey and elephant as symbols of the Democratic and Republican parties.

70 An ABC White House correspondent wrote this about the Reagans: "I hate to say anything bad about [the president's wife] for two reasons. First I think you could look [the president] in the eye and call him anything you wanted, and as long as you were smiling, he'd just laugh. But suggest the slightest imperfection in his wife, and he'll go for you with fire in his eyes. Second, I like [the president's wife]." Who was the newsman?

Answers

① *John F. Kennedy. He held the first live televised news conference on January 25, 1961, five days after taking office.*

② *President Dwight Eisenhower. In 1955 his news conferences were filmed and later aired on television and on newsreels.*

③ *Franklin D. Roosevelt at the 1939 New York World's Fair.*

④ *"All in the Family."*

⑤ *Spiro Agnew in 1968.*

⑥ *Walter Cronkite.*

⑦ *"Roots" by Alex Hailey. With an audience of about 130 million, the week-long series sparked interest among blacks to trace their roots to Africa.*

⑧ *Father Charles Coughlin. In 1942 the government halted the publication of* Social Justice, *his weekly anti-Semitic paper, charging that it violated the Espionage Act of 1917.*

⑨ *Horace Greeley.*

⑩ *Lyndon Baines John-*
son. Many considered this bizarre behavior for a
chief executive.

⑪ *(a)* Playboy *magazine,*
(b) Robert Scheer of The Los Angeles Times.

⑫ *The swimming pool.*

⑬ *Christine Craft. The*
thirty-eight-year-old woman charged that she was de-
moted because management believed her to be "too
old, unattractive, and not deferential to men." Two
separate juries decided in her favor, one awarding
her $500,000 and the other $325,000, but both were
overruled on appeal. The U.S. Supreme Court re-
fused to consider her case.

⑭ *Eastern Europe. Ford*
and Carter participated in two televised debates dur-
ing the 1976 campaign. Carter responded to Ford's
slip by saying that he would like to see how descen-
dants of Poles, Czechs, and Hungarians would re-
spond to that statement.

⑮ *"Death Valley Days,"*
and "The General Electric Theatre."

⑯ *(a) 1976, (b) Republi-*
can—Kansas senator Robert Dole; Democrat—Min-
nesota senator Walter F. Mondale.

⑰ *George Gallup. In 1935 he created the American Institute of Public Opinion and the Gallup Poll, still used today despite his death in 1984.*

⑱ *William Lloyd Garrison. He used* The Liberator *to advance the abolitionist cause.*

⑲ *Lyndon Baines Johnson. Bill Moyers was his press secretary.*

⑳ *Gore Vidal. His district was such a Republican stronghold that he lost despite the fact that he received more votes that year than any Democratic candidate since 1910.*

㉑ *Eleanor Roosevelt. She also wrote a daily syndicated column, "My Day."*

㉒ *(a) General William C. Westmoreland. (b) Mike Wallace. Just days before the case was supposed to go to a jury, the general dismissed the suit after agreeing to settle out of court.*

㉓ *(a) The Fairness Doctrine. (b) The FCC dropped the policy, stating that it could possibly be unconstitutional because it gave the government control over what went out over the airwaves.*

㉔ *Daniel Schorr.*

(25) *Lyndon Johnson. The commercial focused on a young girl counting the petals of a flower as she plucked them. Her voice faded as a male announcer counted backwards from ten. An explosion obliterated the picture of the girl when the announcer reached zero. The commercial ended with the words, "These are the stakes, to make a world in which all of God's children can live or go into the dark. The stakes are too high for you to stay at home." Then there was a plug for Lyndon Johnson.*

(26) *Norman Mailer.*

(27) *Jimmy Breslin. He received more votes than his friend, the mayoral candidate, but still lost.*

(28) *Author Robert Penn Warren wrote* All the King's Men.

(29) *"The Smothers Brothers Comedy Hour," starring Dick and Tom Smothers.*

(30) *Pete Seeger. This was his first* TV *appearance in seventeen years after being blacklisted for his outspoken political stands. The song that met with CBS disfavor was about a soldier in 1942 who was ordered to walk into a body of water without knowing its depth, causing him to drown.*

③¹ *John Quincy Adams.
Reporter Anne Royall took advantage of the fact that
the president went "skinny dipping" in the Potomac
River on warm mornings.*

③² *Van Doren won
$129,000 on the television show "Twenty-One."*

③³ *Woodrow Wilson.*

③⁴ *Theodore White. The*
Making of the President, 1960 *remained on the*

*best-seller list for almost a year and was followed by
sequels in 1964, 1968 and 1972, as well as* Breach
of Faith: The Fall of Richard Nixon. *White was a
reporter for about forty years, writing for such pub-
lications as* Time *and* Collier's *magazines.*

㉟ *Bob Woodward and
Carl Bernstein. The book was* The Final Days.

㊱ All the President's
Men *(which is also the title of another Woodward
and Bernstein book). Robert Redford played Bob
Woodward and Dustin Hoffman took the part of Carl
Bernstein.*

㊲ *Charlie Chaplin. The
U.S. government accused Chaplin of having Communist leanings. While traveling in Europe, he was
told that hearings into his personal and political life
would be held before he could return to the U.S. as
a resident. (Although he had lived in the United
States for over forty years, he was not a citizen).
Rather than subject himself and his family (fourth
wife Oona and their children) to such scrutiny, he
moved to Switzerland.*

㊳ *Jimmy Carter and Ron-
ald Reagan debated in 1980 in Cleveland, Ohio.
Reagan made the two statements.*

㊴ *(a) Actual malice. The
Court said that, for a public official to win damages*

in a libel suit, the publication would have to print it "with knowledge that it was false or with reckless disregard for whether it was false or not."

(40) *Alexander Hamilton and John Jay published* The New York Evening Post.

(41) *Dwight Eisenhower.*

(42) *William Taft, Warren Harding, and John F. Kennedy.*

(43) *Warren Harding.*

(44) *United Press International (UPI). Some Americans began celebrating on November 7, 1918, when a UPI reporter erroneously reported that the armistice had been signed.*

(45) *President Jimmy Carter. The campaign manager, Tim Kraft, was cleared of the charges in March 1981.*

(46) *Harry S Truman.*

(47) *Jimmy Carter. A White House aide recommended the new image.*

(48) *CBS. The network covered the election of Franklin D. Roosevelt and Herbert Hoover in 1932.*

(49) *(a) Harry S Truman, (b) 1948.*

(50) *1952. Republican Dwight Eisenhower ran against Democrat Adlai Stevenson.*

(51) *In a model kitchen on display at the United States national exhibition in Moscow.*

(52) *Ariel Sharon. Although the jury felt the author of the article was irresponsible and the statement unfounded,* Time *was found not guilty of libel because the article was run in good faith.*

(53) *Garry Trudeau. This was the first Pulitzer given for best editorial cartooning.*

(54) *Harry VonZell. The announcer and actor is best remembered for his roles on "The George Burns and Gracie Allen Show."*

(55) *Charles Kuralt.*

(56) *"The MacNeil/Lehrer Report." Robert MacNeil and James Lehrer are the cohosts.*

(57) *William Safire. He wrote* Before the Fall: An Inside View of the Pre-Watergate White House *and a novel,* Full Disclosure.

(58) *Dan Rather of CBS.*

⑤⑨ *(a) Shana Alexander.*

⑥⓪ *(b) Russell Baker.*

⑥① *Edward R. Murrow. He is best known for his radio coverage of World War II, moving on to television reporting and a CBS vice presidency.*

⑥② *1(e), 2(d), 3(f), 4(c), 5(g), 6(b), 7(a), 8(h).*

⑥③ *1(f), 2(d), 3(b), 4(c), 5(e), 6(a).*

⑥④ *(a)* General Motors, *and (b)* Unsafe at Any Speed.

⑥⑤ *Daniel Ellsberg. He was indicted in 1971 for theft, espionage, and conspiracy; but the charges were later dismissed.*

⑥⑥ *(a)* Harriet Beecher Stowe. *(b)* Uncle Tom's Cabin.

⑥⑦ *Ralph David Abernathy. He was an organizer of the 1955 Montgomery bus boycott and took over the presidency of the Southern Christian Leadership Conference after King's death.*

⑥⑧ *Allen Ginsberg.*

⑥⑨ *Thomas Nast. As political cartoonist for* Harper's Weekly, *his caricatures of the Democratic donkey and Republican elephant first appeared in 1874. His cartoons of Boss Tweed and Tammany Hall also helped expose the corruption of New York City politics in 1871.*

⑦⓪ *Sam Donaldson.*

Scandals

The *power and money* that go along with becoming an elected official sometimes expose politicians to temptations, often leading to embarrassment and scandal.

Here are questions about some of the better-known scandals, most not taught in high school and college political science classes. Some familiar scandals are not included in this book (like Thomas Jefferson's alleged romance with one of his slaves), because they're more legend than fact. But we've tried to include questions here about actual affairs and incidents that created scandals in politics. Are you familiar with them?

❶ Name the congressman from Harlem who was excluded not only from his House seat but also from the chairmanship of a powerful House committee in 1967, after a panel concluded that he had pocketed government money.

❷ In 1918, after discovering love letters between her husband and his mistress, Eleanor Roosevelt is said to have issued an ultimatum: Stop seeing this other woman or she would file for divorce. Who was the "other woman"?

❸ Who was President Reagan's secretary of the interior who quickly ended his career in 1983 by describing one of his federal environmental commissions as including a "black, a woman, two Jews, and a cripple"?

❹ Upon the death of this president, rumors flew that his First Lady had poisoned him. Who was he?

❺ Thomas Jefferson was noted for his unfailing devotion to his wife Martha during their ten-year marriage, and he vowed never to remarry after her death. But prior to their marriage, he was very much attracted to married women. In 1768 Jefferson allegedly began an affair with the wife of one of his best friends. Who was she: (a) Betsey Walker, (b) Sarah Bennett, or (c) Lucille F. Bowman?

6 Who was the first member of the U.S. House of Representatives to declare his homosexuality on the House floor, yet went on to win reelection in Massachusetts: (a) Representative Thomas Whiteman, (b) Representative Gary Studds, or (c) Representative Carl Russell?

7 During the early 1980s the Environmental Protection Agency was charged with carrying on "sweetheart deals" with some of the country's most flagrant polluters. Name the administrator of the Superfund, the EPA program for cleaning up toxic wastes, who was under investigation for providing special favors for polluting companies. Was it (a) Janet Todd, (b) Rita Lavelle, or (c) Susan LaVigno?

8 The Grant administration was plagued by major scandals. In 1872 it was made public that some members of the administration and Congress were receiving bribes to halt a congressional investigation of the Union Pacific Railroad. Name the scandal.

9 Here's a follow-up question. Who was Grant's vice president who lost his job as a result of the scandal?

10 Two corrupt specula-
tors attempted to corner the gold market in 1869,
creating a panic and causing "Black Friday" on
Wall Street. Who were they?

11 Here's a two-parter:
(a) Name the congressman who had a "secretary"
who could neither type nor file, and (b) name the
secretary who eventually cost him his political career by revealing their illicit affair.

12 Who was the governor
of Arizona who was impeached in 1988 after the
state senate convicted him of illegally lending state
funds to his own car dealership and for obstructing
a grand jury investigation into death threats made
against one of his former staff members?

13 General Dwight Eisen-
hower allegedly became romantically involved
with an Englishwoman who served as his driver in
London during World War II. The former model
and actress wrote a "tell-all" book in 1975. Who
was she?

14 George Washington
married Martha Dandridge Custis, one of Virginia's wealthiest women, yet some believe she was
not his first true love. Here's a two-parter: (a) Who
would he have preferred to marry, and (b) why
didn't he?

⑮ Who was President Ford's secretary of agriculture who was forced to resign because of his raucous racial jokes?

⑯ In 1981 a Playboy model and Capitol Hill lobbyist allegedly attempted to gain the legislative support she needed for her clients with her own little "sex, lies, and videotape" operation. Who was this lobbyist: (a) Beth Samuels, (b) Paula Parkinson, or (c) Cindy Benjamin?

⑰ The woman in the previous question became well-known when it was reported that in 1980 she spent a weekend in Florida with three Republican congressmen. She claimed one congressman from Indiana had made improper advances, which she said she rejected. The accusation became particularly important several years later. Who was the congressman?

⑱ What former Miss America was New York City's Cultural Affairs Commissioner during Mayor Ed Koch's administration until she was handed an indictment for attempting to bribe a New York judge?

⑲ Who was President Eisenhower's chief of staff (and former governor of New Hampshire) who was forced to resign after a congressional committee investigated charges that he had accepted bribes worth more than one million dollars?

20 The controversial governor-general of New York appeared at the opening of the 1702 New York assembly dressed in a hoop skirt much like those of his cousin Queen Anne. He answered the quizzical stares with the following remarks: "You are all very stupid people not to see the propriety of it all. In this place, and on this occasion, I represent a woman, and in all respects, I ought to represent her as faithfully as I can." Can you name this governor-general?

21 Name the Maryland governor convicted of mail fraud and racketeering in 1977.

22 President Truman's secretary of defense could not take the pressures of his governmental duties and ended his own life. Was he: (a) Donald Manes, (b) James Forrestal, or (c) Clarence Saunders?

23 This eighteenth-century politician created quite a stir when he took a common-law wife. This was magnified when she agreed to raise the illegitimate child he had fathered with another woman. Not only did he have several extramarital affairs into his seventies, but he wrote about them. Who was this politician?

24 A former chief enforcement officer of the Securities and Exchange Commission in the Reagan administration resigned after the public learned that he violently abused his wife. Was he: (a) Walter White, (b) John M. Fedders, or (c) Anthony Comstock?

25 A contender for the presidential nomination said: "I made a mistake in my personal life. I have also insisted, as I think I have a right to, that my mistake in my personal life be put against the mistakes of this administration... selling arms to terrorists, lying to Congress, shredding documents." (a) Who made the statement, and (b) what was the mistake to which he was referring?

26 What friend and former employee of President Lyndon Johnson became the focus of a hot scandal in 1963 and 1964 when he was charged with influence peddling in the Senate?

27 The Iran-Contra scandal involved the secret shipping of weapons by the United States to the "contra" rebels fighting the Nicaraguan Sandinista government in exchange for the release of American hostages in Lebanon. The key figure implicated in the scandal eventually became a folk hero, and more or less the scapegoat for others as high up as the president. Name him.

28 President Reagan's national security adviser and White House chief of staff were two other casualties of the Iran-Contra scandal. Name the two men who resigned.

29 What was the infamous "Abscam" scandal of 1980?

30 Where did the word "Abscam" come from?

31 Who was the wife of a South Carolinian congressman who created a scandal by appearing half nude in *Playboy Magazine* after her husband was embroiled in his own scandal—Abscam?

32 In 1988 President Bush's nomination for secretary of defense was turned down in part because of his reputation for heavy drinking and stepping out with the ladies. Who was this former senator and chairman of the Armed Services Committee?

33 During the presidential campaign of 1952, vice presidential candidate Richard Nixon was accused of dipping into an expense fund provided by wealthy supporters and using it for personal expenditures. On national television, Nixon dramatically denied any wrongdoing, saying he had received only one gift and "we're going to keep it!" What was the gift?

34 Billy Carter caused political trouble for his brother Jimmy when it was revealed that he was an agent for an African nation, from which he received payments or so-called "loans" totalling over $200,000. Name the country.

35 While the Nixon administration was attempting to stay afloat during the Watergate fiasco, Vice President Spiro Agnew was having his own problems. Under investigation for several criminal violations, to what charge did he ultimately plead no contest?

36 A Democratic presidential candidate in the late nineteenth century was accused of having fathered a child out of wedlock. The Republicans jumped on this indiscretion as a campaign issue, marching around New York City chanting, "Ma, ma, where's my pa?" The Democrats turned the political pun around, responding with, "gone to the White House, ha-ha-ha." Their retort was clever enough to help send him there. Who was he?

37 The 1884 election involved just about the dirtiest politicking in U.S. history. Not only did Grover Cleveland have skeletons in his closet, but his opponent was known for under the table dealings in the Crédit Mobilier scandal. Who was this candidate who defeated incumbent president Chester Arthur for the spot on the Republican presidential ticket?

38 Regardless of the ethics involved, Ronald Reagan clearly had an advantage over his Democratic opponent in the 1980 presidential debates—he managed to get his hands on Jimmy Carter's debate briefing book. What names were given to the scandal of (a) the book falling into the hands of the Republican campaign committee, and (b) Reagan and his aides actually using the material to prepare for the debate? (Hint: After Watergate, everything became a "gate.")

39 Name the Washington, D.C. mayor who was arrested in 1989 during a videotaped FBI drug sting, catching him in the act of smoking crack cocaine.

40 The secretary of the interior during the Harding administration was forced to resign and was convicted of criminal charges for his part in the Teapot Dome Scandal of 1922. Name him.

41 Speaking of the Teapot Dome Scandal, how did it get its name?

42 A New York City public official built a corrupt and massive political machine in the mid-1800s, controlling just about every aspect of city government, and creating a financial disaster for the city after bilking it of millions. (a) Who was he, and (b) what was the name of the political machine he ran?

43 President Andrew Jackson believed the death of his wife, Rachel Donelson Robards, was caused in part by the brutal press attacks regarding her morality and character—charges that she had committed adultery. On what were these charges based?

44 In 1831 President Jackson's cabinet fell apart because of the harsh feelings some members had toward the wife of the secretary of war, a woman with a rather seedy reputation. (a) Name the secretary of war and his wife. (b) What was the incident called?

45 In 1987 a U.S. congressman from Georgia was involved in a drug money laundering scheme, resulting in a perjury conviction. He ran for reelection in 1988, losing to the actor who once played "Cooter" on the television show "Dukes of Hazard." Name the two politicians.

46 One First Lady had a long-standing addiction to drugs and alcohol, but her problems didn't become known to the public until after she left the White House. She successfully underwent treatment at a rehab center and later helped raise money for a similar facility. (a) Name the former First Lady, and (b) where is the clinic located?

47 At one time, it was rumored that First Lady Mamie Eisenhower had a drinking problem. What disease did she have that has symptoms that might lead people to suspect that she was an alcoholic?

48 Koreagate was a scandal that shook the country during the late 1970s. It involved the bribing by South Koreans of over one hundred U.S. congressmen in an effort to keep U.S. troops militarily involved in their country. Name the South Korean who headed the influence-peddling scheme.

49 Here's a follow-up question: One former U.S. congressman pled guilty to helping the South Korean mentioned above in his elaborate influence-peddling scheme, thus becoming the first congressman to admit he had been involved in illegal activities when he was in office. Who was he?

50 Who was President Carter's director of the U.S. Office of Management and Budget, who resigned under a cloud of illegal banking charges?

51 President Carter also had a chief of staff who was under investigation for cocaine use. Who was he?

52 Who was the cabinet member in George Washington's administration who became involved in a sexual blackmail scheme?

53 New York City's mayor, "Gentleman Jimmy," was popular with his constituents, not only for the subway and sanitation systems he created for the city, but also for his suave "uptown" style. This all came crashing down in 1932 when an investigation and hearing revealed he was receiving gifts under the table. He resigned in September of that year. Who was he? (Hint: He was not related to the actor in the TV series "Good Times.")

54 Scandal caused this U.S. Speaker of the House to resign in mid-term—the first ever to have done so. Who was he?

55 Who was the senior member of the House of Representatives who was unanimously censured in 1979 after admitting to using public monies to pay his mortgage, alimony, car, and other personal expenses?

56 The U.S. attorney general under President Reagan was charged with conflict-of-interest violations, tax evasion and accepting bribes from a government contractor, Wedtech. He resigned before his guilt or innocence was determined. Name him.

57 President Nixon probably could have continued his cover-up in the Watergate affair had it not been for the taped conversations that took place in the White House Oval Office. Who revealed to the Watergate investigating committee that the taping system existed?

58 Any hopes Ted Kennedy may have had to make a run for the 1972 Democratic presidential nomination were dashed on July 18, 1967, when he drove his car off Dike Bridge on Martha's Vineyard, killing his female companion. (a) Where on Martha's Vineyard did the accident occur, and (b) who was the woman killed in the accident?

59 When one of the most influential men in Nixon's administration was sentenced to prison for his role in Watergate, he remarked to reporters: "It could have been worse. They could have sentenced me to spend the rest of my life with Martha." (a) Who was he, (b) what was his position in the administration, and (c) who was Martha?

60 Follow-up question: One of the tapes involved a June 20, 1972, conversation between Chief of Staff H. R. Haldeman and the president, just three days after the Watergate arrests. Nixon's credibility suffered further when it was discovered that a portion of that tape had been erased. (a) How long was the infamous gap on the subpoenaed tape, and (b) who was Nixon's secretary who admitted to having erased about five minutes of the tape?

61 Fanne Foxe, a striptease artist in the nation's capital, gained notoriety in 1974 because of her affair with the energetic sixty-five-year-old chairman of the House Ways and Means Committee. Who was the congressman?

62 President Bush's son, Neil Bush, was director of a Denver savings and loan institution that failed, one of many in the S&L bailout scandal of the late 1980s. Bush was accused of violating conflict of interest rules, and the seizure of his S&L in 1988 cost taxpayers approximately one billion dollars. Name the S&L.

Answers

① Adam Clayton Powell. His seat was restored two years later in 1969, but he was denied his seniority and fined $25,000. In June 1969 the Supreme Court ruled that his exclusion from the House was unconstitutional, but he lost his reelection bid in 1970.

② Lucy Page Mercer. She married Winthrop Rutherfurd in 1920, but she and FDR later resumed their affair. Lucy was at his bedside when he died of a stroke in 1945 in Warm Springs, Georgia.

③ James G. Watt. This was not Watt's first impropriety. In 1982 the General

Accounting Office ordered him to pay back federal government monies he had used to throw two private parties.

④ *Warren Harding. He died unexpectedly in August 1923 while in San Francisco on his way back from a trip to Alaska. The doctors concluded that he had died from a stroke, but some historians theorize that his wife, Florence Kling DeWolfe, poisoned him because of his infidelities. The cause of death could not be confirmed because the First Lady would not allow an autopsy.*

⑤ *(a) Betsey Walker. However, whether Jefferson and Walker actually had an affair continues to be controversial. Some historians believe the scandal was created by the Federalist press during Jefferson's first term.*

⑥ *(b) Representative Gary Studds. In 1982 a massive investigation was undertaken into sexual, homosexual, and drug activities between congressmen and teenagers serving as pages on the Hill. The investigation did not end in any prosecutions, but it caused the humiliation of two congressmen: Gary Studds and Daniel Crane. Illinois congressman Daniel Crane, a married man with six children, confessed to having sexual relations with a female teenage page, a revelation costing him reelection in 1984.*

⑦ *(b) Rita Lavelle. She was ultimately found guilty of perjury for her testimony before two House committees and sentenced to six months in prison and five years probation with community service.*

⑧ *The Crédit Mobilier scandal. Acting as the construction company of the Union Pacific Railroad, Crédit Mobilier of America padded its construction costs, bilking the railroad of enormous amounts of money.*

Massachusetts Congressman Oakes Ames, heavily involved in the scandal, saw that a government investigation was inevitable. Hoping to forestall the inquiry, he "sold" Crédit Mobilier stock at half its value to members of the administration and legislators.

⑨ *Vice President Schuyler Colfax was accused of accepting the stock bribe in 1872 while he served as House Speaker five years earlier. Grant dropped him from the ticket in his re-election bid, selecting Senator Henry Wilson instead.*

⑩ *Jay Gould and Jim Fisk. In addition to their underhanded attempts to corner the gold market, they became wealthy men by manipulating the stock in the Erie Railroad.*

⑪ *(a) Wayne Hays. (b) Elizabeth Ray. Hays confessed in May 1976 that he and Ray had engaged in a "personal relationship."*

He also accused her of blackmailing him, demanding $1,000 in exchange for her silence. He came forward with these revelations after Ray, angry because Hays had married another employee, went to the Washington Post *with her story. Hays' political career unraveled through the exposure, and he eventually resigned after the House Ethics Committee announced it would hold public hearings.*

(12) *Evan Mecham. A controversial figure, he was noted for his comments and jokes against just about every minority group in the United States. One of his first official acts as governor was to cancel Martin Luther King Day as an official state holiday.*

(13) *Kay Summersby. Eisenhower supposedly ended the two-year relationship in 1944 when it became apparent the extramarital affair could damage his future in the military and, perhaps, political arena.*

(14) *(a) Sally Fairfax, the young bride of Washington's good friend and next-door neighbor. (b) Divorce was out of the question in colonial times, so Washington set out to find a bride of his own, continuing to express his love for Sally through letters even on the eve of his wedding.*

(15) *Earl Butz. A racist joke he told to singers Pat Boone and Sonny Bono on an*

airplane during the 1976 presidential election was told in the presence of John Dean III of Watergate fame, who was working for Rolling Stone Magazine. *The joke was printed without attribution, but when it became clear that Butz was the jokester, the political heat became too much, and he resigned.*

⑯ *(b) Paula Parkinson. The Justice Department investigated charges that she was trading sexual favors for congressmen's votes, but ended their inquiry after finding nothing to substantiate the accusations.*

⑰ *J. Danforth Quayle. When he became Bush's choice for a vice presidential running mate, the news media reported Parkinson's allegations. Quayle denied them vehemently.*

⑱ *Bess Myerson, Miss America of 1945. Myerson was accused of having given a job to the daughter of the judge in exchange for a reduction in alimony payments in the divorce case of her beau, wealthy businessman Andy Capasso. Myerson was acquitted of the charges, but was arrested in 1988 for shoplifting. She pled guilty and was fined.*

⑲ *Sherman Adams. It was alleged that he received expensive gifts, including an oriental rug, a tractor, and a miniature golf course, in return for using his influence with the Fed-*

eral Trade Commission and the Securities and Exchange Commission on behalf of his old friend, Bernard Goldfine. Goldfine, an industrialist and textile manufacturer, was under investigation by Congress for violating manufacturing laws. Despite support from Eisenhower and his continual denials of any wrongdoing, Adams resigned in September 1958 to end further humiliation for the Republican party.

⑳ Lord Cornbury. Not only was he a transvestite, but he was a corrupt leader, embezzling funds from the New York assembly, illegally selling large tracts of lands to friends, collecting taxes to build a home for himself, and taking kickbacks and payoffs. By 1708 Lord Cornbury became so offensive that Queen Anne removed him from office.

㉑ Marvin Mandel. It took 113 hours of deliberation for the jury to find Mandel and five co-defendants guilty of illegal activities. The governor was found guilty of accepting over $350,000 in bribes from five businessmen and politicians. Mandel, sentenced to four years in prison, was automatically suspended from office.

㉒ (b) James Forrestal. During his tenure as the first secretary of defense, the armed services were being unified and there was infighting among the army, navy, and air force about status and allocations. The stress became too much

*for Forrestal, causing him to exhibit strange para-
noid behavior. He resigned and admitted himself to
Bethesda Naval Hospital for psychiatric treatment.
Two months later he leapt from the hospital window
to his death.*

㉓ *Benjamin Franklin. In*
his Poor Richard's Almanac, *Franklin commented
that "where there's marriage without love, there will
be love without marriage." Most history students
were never taught that Franklin fell "in love" often.*

㉔ *(b) John M. Fedders.
The* Wall Street Journal *wrote a sensational exposé
in February of 1985, stating that Fedders admitted
during divorce proceedings that he had beaten his
wife on seven occasions. Mrs. Fedders filed for divorce in 1985 and wrote a book,* Shattered Dreams,
*describing her life as a battered wife. John Fedders
demanded a share in the profits, but a Maryland
judge denied his request.*

㉕ *(a) Gary Hart. (b) Dur-
ing the 1988 presidential primary campaign, Hart
withdrew from the race upon the revelation that he
was having an affair with Donna Rice, a twenty-
nine-year-old model and actress. After the dust settled, he attempted to reenter the race, stating that if
he was elected, he wouldn't be the first president who
had committed adultery. But the affair had been too
damaging, and in March 1988, he withdrew from
the race.*

㉖ *Bobby Baker. In 1955, when Johnson was Senate majority leader, he hired Baker as his secretary. Over the next eight years, Baker amassed a personal fortune said to be around $2,225,000. His business dealings became the focus of a Senate investigation, and in 1967 Baker was convicted of tax evasion, theft, and conspiracy to defraud the government, subsequently serving seventeen months in prison.*

㉗ *Oliver North. In 1989 he was convicted on three felony charges and acquitted on nine others. He received a three-year suspended sentence and a fine of $150,000.*

㉘ *National Security Advisor John Poindexter and White House Chief of Staff Donald Regan.*

㉙ *The Abscam sting operation involved FBI agents posing as Arab sheiks, making illegal deals with congressmen. Thirty-one public officials were investigated, resulting in the convictions of seven congressmen on bribery and conspiracy charges. The last to be convicted was Senator Harrison A. Williams of New Jersey who gained the distinction of being the first United States senator to be convicted of criminal charges while in office since 1905 and only the fourth in United States history.*

㉚ *The word "Abscam" is the shortened form of Arab scam.*

③① *Rita Jenrette. Her husband, Congressman John W. Jenrette, Jr. was convicted of bribery and conspiracy in October 1980 for his part in Abscam. The next year, Mrs. Jenrette appeared in* Playboy *Magazine and spoke openly to the press about her estranged, and later divorced, husband's alleged alcohol and womanizing problems.*

③② *John Tower. This was the first time in thirty years that a president's cabinet nomination was rejected.*

③③ *The gift was a dog. Nixon's vehement denial was made in his famous "Checkers" speech.*

③④ *Libya. Investigations by the Justice Department and a Senate committee concluded that he had not done anything illegal, but had lied about the payments. This incident did little to help the already waning popularity of President Carter, who was up for reelection.*

③⑤ *Income tax evasion. Agnew had also been charged with bribery, conspiracy, and extortion involving illegal kickbacks for government contracts while serving as Maryland's governor and as vice president. In 1973 he entered into a plea bargain arrangement—pleading no contest to tax evasion and resigning his position as vice president in return for not being tried for the more serious charges. He received a three-year probated sentence and a $10,000 fine.*

㊱ *Grover Cleveland. The bachelor president was not sure whether he had in fact fathered little Oscar, but decided to take the credit and pay child support because the other possible fathers were married. These charges could have easily brought an end to his political career, but his openness and instructions to his campaign staff to tell the truth took the wind out of his opponents' sails.*

㊲ *James Blaine. The charismatic candidate could probably have overcome the bad press about the Crédit Mobilier and gone on to win the 1884 presidency had he not made other political blunders during the campaign.*

㊳ *(a) Briefingate and (b) Debategate. These scandals never reached the notoriety level of Watergate.*

㊴ *Mayor Marion Barry. The jury convicted him on only one misdemeanor cocaine possession charge, acquitted him on another, and deadlocked on twelve other charges. Prior to the sting operation, Barry had denied the use of drugs on many occasions.*

㊵ *Albert Fall. He was accused of secretly leasing government oil fields to private companies without competitive bidding in return for illegal loans. Suspicion against Fall mounted when he spent $170,000 on his New Mexico ranch with an annual salary of only $42,000. He* *was eventually convicted, receiving a one-year sentence and a $100,000 fine.*

④① *The oil fields that were at the center of the scandal were located on Teapot Dome, a government naval oil reserve. The reserve was near a rock formation supposedly shaped like a large teapot; thus, the Teapot Dome Scandal.*

④② *(a) He was William M. (Boss) Tweed, and (b) he ran Tammany Hall. Tweed was indicted for forgery and grand larceny, and died in prison.*

④③ *When Jackson and Rachel married, they were unaware that her divorce from Lewis Robards was not yet final. Robards learned of his wife's invalid marriage, and sued for divorce, claiming that she had committed adultery. The president and Rachel corrected their mistake by remarrying in 1794, but the accusations of adultery continued to follow them and became a campaign issue in 1828.*

④④ *(a) Secretary of War John Eaton and Peggy O'Neal Eaton, (b) the "petticoat war." Her father owned an inn and tavern during Mrs. Eaton's teenage years, and she gained a reputation for helping to "entertain" the male guests. She was never able to shake that reputation and gossip, even after her marriage to John Eaton. The couple was ostracized by Washington society, and there was a strong faction among cabinet members calling for his resignation. He and Secretary of State Martin Van Buren stepped down to enable Jackson to reorganize his cabinet, and the other members followed suit.*

(45) *Pat Swindall (some felt the name was appropriate). Former actor and Democratic candidate Ben Jones beat Swindall in 1988.*

(46) *(a) Betty Ford, and (b) Long Beach, California.*

(47) *She suffered from an inner ear malady called Meniere's disease and often experienced dizziness, causing talk around Washington that she was a bit tipsy from alcohol.*

(48) *Park Tong Sun. Defending his actions, he told Congress, "I thought I was taking part in the American political process. So far as I was concerned, I was helping congressional friends who were loyal to me." Charges against Park were eventually dropped.*

(49) *Richard T. Hanna. The Democrat from California was sentenced to six to thirty months, serving just over one year.*

(50) *Bert Lance. He was indicted on thirty-three counts of banking violations, charges that were so complicated that the govern-*

*ment investigation lasted three years and cost the
taxpayers seven million dollars. He managed to
avoid prison, but paid a $50,000 fine and was pro-
hibited from holding a position in a federally insured
banking institution.*

⑤ *Hamilton Jordan. A
special prosecutor was appointed to investigate the
alleged use of cocaine, charges that were eventually
dropped after a special grand jury concluded that
insufficient evidence existed. Earlier, Jordan had
brought embarrassment to the White House with
newspaper reports that he spit a drink on a woman
while at a bar. In a March 1978 news conference,
President Carter "discounted" the reports.*

⑤ *Alexander Hamilton.
Two con artists, Maria and James Reynolds, devised
a plot to extort cash from Hamilton in exchange for
sexual favors. The scheme was successful and Hamilton eventually confessed his indiscretions to three
congressmen. The affair remained a secret for six
years until it was revealed in volumes V and VI of
James Callender's* History of the U.S. for the Year
1796, *published in 1797.*

⑤ *Jimmy Walker.*

⑤ *Jim Wright. He was ac-
cused by the House Ethics Committee of unethically
receiving gifts from a Texas businessman. Although
maintaining his innocence, he resigned his House*

seat and, of course, the Speakership when the press coverage became unrelenting in May 1989.

55 *Charles Diggs. The Michigan Democrat was convicted of filing false congressional payroll forms and was sentenced to three years in prison. He resigned after his censuring and began serving time. Diggs was the first representative to be censured in fifty-eight years.*

56 *Edwin Meese.*

57 *Alexander Butterfield. The former deputy assistant to Nixon shocked the nation when he testified before a Senate committee in 1973 that the president had been secretly taping conversations on a recording system in the Oval Office.*

58 *(a) Chappaquiddick, and (b) Mary Jo Kopechne.*

59 *(a) John Mitchell. (b) He was a former U.S. attorney general. (c) Martha was his wife, a rather outspoken woman who accused her husband of drugging her and holding her prisoner to keep her quiet during the Watergate scandal. Mitchell was paroled in January 1979 after serving nineteen months.*

60 *(a) Eighteen and one half minutes, and (b) Rosemary Wood.*

61 *Wilbur Mills. Foxe allegedly jumped out of Mills' car one night in October*

1974, somehow falling into the Tidal Basin. The police, seeing the incident, arrested Mills, Foxe, and a masseuse also in the car. Foxe used the publicity to her advantage in her striptease career, billing herself as the "Tidal Basin Bombshell." Mills, who commanded a great deal of power in the House, managed to win reelection that November, but the publicity from the continuing affair with Foxe and an alcohol problem took its toll on Mills' career. He withdrew from politics in 1975 at the age of sixty-six.

(62) *The Silverado Bank.*

Famous and
Infamous Words

Abraham Lincoln underestimated the power of his words at Gettysburg in 1863 when he said, "The world will little note, nor long remember, what we say here, but it can never forget what they did here."

Lincoln's remarks, as well as those made by other well-known Americans, have often incensed, incited, and inspired people worldwide. Here are some famous, as well as fun, quotations by politicians, statesmen, and even comedians. See how well you do at identifying them.

❶ Journalist Dorothy Parker of *The New Yorker* magazine was not a big fan of one twentieth-century president. Upon hearing of his death, she replied, "How could they tell?" Who was the president?

❷ President Richard Nixon once said, "This is the greatest week in the history of the world since the creation." What event was he referring to? (Hint: It was *not* Watergate.)

❸ Which Democratic presidential candidate answered his critics by saying: "Republican leaders have not been content with attacks on me, or my wife, or my sons. No, not content with that, they now include my little dog Fala. Fala does resent them. He has not been the same dog since"?

❹ Who said, "Without television, Nixon had it made"? (Hint: He also said, "The medium is the message.")

❺ Which vice president had so little respect for his job that he said, "It isn't worth a pitcher of warm spit"?

❻ Which former president, known for his "plain speaking," defined a statesman as "a politician who has been dead ten or fifteen years"?

❼ Name the humorist who once wrote: "Reader, suppose you were an idiot. And suppose you were a member of Congress. But, I repeat myself."

8 Which president used the following colorful language to explain why he had dismissed General Douglas MacArthur: "I fired him because he wouldn't respect the authority of the President . . . I didn't fire him because he was a dumb son of a bitch, although he was, but that's not against the law for generals. If it was, half to three-quarters of them would be in jail."

9 One president did not attempt to hide his displeasure with his two-term vice president. When asked what major decisions his second-in-command had taken part in, he responded, "If you give me a week, I might think of one." Who were the president and vice president?

10 After the passage of the Kansas-Nebraska Act in 1854, this Illinois senator, sponsor of the controversial legislation, said, "I could travel from Boston to Chicago by the light of my effigies." Who was he?

11 One president committed a major gaffe in 1984 when he said, while checking a radio microphone: "My fellow Americans, I am pleased to tell you that I have signed legislation to outlaw Russia forever. We begin bombing in five minutes." Who was he?

⑫ Which general and future president told U.S. troops: "The eyes of the world are upon you. The hopes and prayers of liberty-loving people everywhere march with you." And, for extra credit, what was the event?

⑬ While on vacation, this legislator was summoned to the White House for a conference regarding the downing of a Korean jetliner by the Soviets. When he asked how the president felt about the incident, the legislator was told: "He's still asleep. He doesn't know about it yet. We'll tell him when he wakes up." (a) Who was the president who needed his sleep, and (b) who was the legislator?

⑭ Who was the U.S. financier and presidential consultant who advised the electorate to "vote for the man who promises least, he'll be the least disappointing"?

⑮ Which news anchor said in 1961 "this is the first Convention of the space age—where a candidate can promise the moon and mean it": (a) Walter Cronkite, (b) Peter Jennings, or (c) David Brinkley?

⑯ Which president had many constituents agreeing with him when he said, "I am not fit for this office and never should have been here"?

17 What politician once told this story to illustrate his perception of the importance of the vice presidency: "Once there were two brothers. One ran away to sea. The other was elected vice president, and nothing was heard of either of them again." Was it (a) Charles Curtis, (b) Lyndon Johnson, or (c) Thomas Marshall?

18 A flamboyant congresswoman from New York had this to say about herself: "I have been described as a tough and noisy woman, a prize fighter, a man-hater, you name it. . . . There are those who say I am impatient, impetuous, uppity, rude, profane, brash, and overbearing." Who was this "self-effacing" legislator?

19 Adlai Stevenson once said this of a certain president, "[He] is the kind of politician who would cut down a redwood tree, then mount the stump for a conservation speech." Which president was he referring to?

20 One president who had a less than liberal view of women, declared: "Sensible and responsible women do not want to vote. The relative positions to be assumed by man and woman in working out of our civilization were assigned long ago by a higher intelligence than ours." Was he (a) John Adams, (b) Grover Cleveland, or (c) Warren Harding?

㉑ Which former twentieth-century president said, "I used to say that politics was the second oldest profession, and I have come to know that it bears a great similarity to the first"?

㉒ A famous early twentieth-century attorney remarked that: "When I was a boy, I was told that anybody could become President of the United States. I am beginning to believe it." Name him.

㉓ One president managed to maintain his sense of humor after an attempt was made on his life, saying to his wife at the hospital, "Honey, I forgot to duck." He also joked with the surgeons saying, "Please tell me you're Republicans." Who was the president?

㉔ Which two-term, early twentieth-century Democratic president said, "Every man who takes office in Washington either grows or swells, and when I give a man an office, I watch him carefully to see whether he is swelling or growing"?

㉕ Which former president once quipped that he received a telegram saying, "Dear _____, don't buy a single vote more than is necessary—I'll be damned if I am going to pay for a landslide." For extra credit, who was the telegram supposedly from?

26 This Republican will be long remembered for his erudite remarks, including, "When people are out of work, unemployment results" and "Business will be better or worse." Who is he?

27 What candidate made these remarks after his third unsuccessful run at the presidency: "I am reminded of the drunk who, when he had been thrown down the stairs of a club for the third time, gathered himself up, and said, 'I am on to those people. They don't want me in there.'"

28 Which president was Tennessee congressman Davy Crockett describing when he said: "He is laced up in corsets, such as women in town wear, and, if possible, tighter than the best of them. It would be difficult to say from his personal appearance, whether he was man or woman, but for his large whiskers. . . ."

29 A First Lady took a beating from the news media when she ordered new china for the White House. Her response:

I did not buy the china! For the press, the china was a symbol of my supposed extravagance. Here, too, the timing was unfortunate. The new White House china was announced on the same day that the Department of Agriculture mistakenly declared ketchup to be acceptable as a vegetable for school lunches. As you can imagine, the columnists and cartoonists had a field day with that one.

Who was the first lady?

30 It's hard to believe but one president was worried about the way his assassin was being treated after the shooting. He ordered the crowd, "Don't let them hurt him." Who was this president?

31 Name the presidential candidate in the 1950s who said, "In America, any boy may become President; and I suppose it is just one of the risks he takes." Was it (a) Dwight Eisenhower, (b) Adlai Stevenson, or (c) Estes Kefauver?

32 This women's rights opponent, apparently not happy with liberal politicians in 1964, said, "America is waiting for an Attorney General who will enforce the law—and a President with the courage to demand that he do so." Who was she?

33 Which president wrote this regarding slavery in Virginia, "I tremble for my country when I reflect that God is just; that his justice cannot sleep forever"?

34 Which former president said this about Gerald Ford, "Gerry is a nice guy, but he played too much football with his helmet off"?

35 Name the Watergate judge who, believing that Nixon should have stood trial instead of being pardoned, said: "If Nixon had had the character of President Eisenhower, or any honest president, this scandal would never have happened. . . . I hope no political party will ever stoop so low as to embrace the likes of Richard Nixon again."

36 Which president told reporters, "I'm not going to say anything terribly important tonight, so you can all put your crayons away"?

37 What comedian once said, "Too bad that all the people who know how to run the country are busy driving taxicabs and cutting hair": (a) George Burns, (b) Jack Benny, or (c) Mort Sahl?

38 Who wrote, "These are the times that try men's souls"?

39 What civil rights leader said, "If a man hasn't discovered something he will die for, he isn't fit to live"?

40 Here's a three-parter: (a) Name the president who said, "Ich bin ein Berliner," (b) explain what it means, and (c) give the occasion when it was said.

41 This president, the first to speak at a nominating convention, made these stirring comments during his acceptance speech: "This is more than a political campaign, it is a call to arms. Give me your help, not to win votes alone, but to win in this crusade to restore America to its own people. I pledge you, I pledge myself, to a new deal for the American people." Who made these comments?

42 Who said, "The only thing to fear is fear itself"?

43 President Harry Truman had a sign on his desk that reminded him of his responsibilities as chief executive. What did it say?

44 Who said, "I am not a crook"?

45 One of our Founding Fathers said, "We must indeed all hang together, or most assuredly, we shall all hang separately." Who made these historic remarks?

46 What president felt so strongly about resolving the energy crisis that he called it "the moral equivalent of war"?

47 Who criticized violent protests by saying, "A rioter with a Molotov cocktail in his hands is not fighting for civil rights any more than a Klansman wearing a sheet and a mask"?

48 This U.S. general left gracefully after being relieved of his command by President Truman, saying these memorable words: "Old soldiers never die; they just fade away." Who was he?

49 What twentieth-century president said: "I never did give anybody hell. I just told the truth, and they thought it was hell."

50 What president was less than accurate when he made this prediction in his inaugural address: "I have no fears for the future of our country. It is bright with hope."

Answers

① *Calvin Coolidge, the country's thirtieth president. Coolidge was very shy and restrained.*

② *Nixon was referring to the first moon landing. He made his comments on July 24, 1969, just four days after the historic event. He told astronauts Neil Armstrong and Edwin Ald-*

rin while they were still in space, "For one priceless moment in the whole history of man, the people of this Earth are truly one."

(3) *Franklin D. Roosevelt.* He was answering charges in 1944 that he spent millions of taxpayers' dollars by deploying a destroyer to retrieve his dog, Fala, who had been left behind on the Aleutian Islands. Maybe Richard Nixon picked up on this unique use of a dog to gain sympathy in his 1952 "Checkers" speech.

(4) *Marshall McLuhan.* This comment by the Canadian communications specialist was a prime example of the "Medium is the message," that is, the information presented is not as important as the way it is communicated. Nixon was far less attractive and charismatic than John F. Kennedy, and it is believed Nixon's popularity suffered because of his TV appearance during the presidential debates of 1960.

(5) *John Nance Garner.* He served as vice president during Franklin D. Roosevelt's first two terms.

(6) *Harry S Truman.*

(7) *Mark Twain.*

(8) *Harry S Truman.*

(9) *President Dwight Eisenhower and Vice President Richard Nixon.*

⑩ *Stephen A. Douglas. The act created the territories of Kansas and Nebraska and reopened the whole issue of slavery in the territories by giving the residents the right to decide whether they wanted to allow slavery or not.*

⑪ *Ronald Reagan. The Soviet press agency TASS called the president's comments "unprecedently hostile toward the USSR and dangerous to the cause of peace." The State Department responded by accusing the Soviets of blowing the whole incident out of proportion.*

⑫ *Dwight Eisenhower. He made these remarks to the American troops on June 6, 1944—D-Day—when the Allies successfully invaded Normandy.*

⑬ *(a) President Ronald Reagan. (b) "Tip" O'Neill, Speaker of the House from 1977 to 1987.*

⑭ *Bernard Baruch.*

⑮ *(c) David Brinkley. One of the most respected TV journalists in the United States, he was one-half of the Huntley-Brinkley news broadcasting team from 1956 to 1970.*

⑯ *Warren Harding. Although he served only twenty-nine months, his administration was filled with scandals, and he is considered by many historians to have been the worst president in history.*

⑰ *(c) Thomas Marshall, vice president to Woodrow Wilson. Marshall was known for his sense of humor. While serving as presiding officer of the Senate, he helped break the insufferable monotony of Senator Joseph Bristow's lengthy comments on "What This Country Needs" by remarking, "What this country needs is a really good five-cent cigar."*

⑱ *Bella Abzug. Most easily recognized for her big hats and her aggressive demeanor, Abzug was a major opponent of the Vietnam War and has long been a supporter of the Equal Rights Amendment and other women's causes.*

⑲ *Richard Nixon.*

⑳ *(b) Grover Cleveland. He was quoted in* The Ladies Home Journal *in April 1905.*

㉑ *Ronald Reagan.*

㉒ *Clarence Darrow. He is best known for his defense of John Scopes who was on trial for teaching Darwin's theory of evolution.*

㉓ *Ronald Reagan. John Hinckley tried to kill the president outside the Washington Hilton Hotel. The president's injuries were not serious, but Press Secretary Jim Brady, who was also shot, was left permanently disabled.*

(24) *Woodrow Wilson.*

(25) *The former president was John F. Kennedy. The telegram was supposedly sent by Joseph Kennedy. Patriarch of the Kennedy Clan, he was a millionaire businessman.*

(26) *Calvin Coolidge.*

(27) *William Jennings Bryan. He ran unsuccessfully in the presidential elections of 1896, 1900, and 1908.*

(28) *Martin Van Buren. Crockett considered him to be an English "dandy," quite unlike retiring president Andrew Jackson under whom Crockett served during the Creek War.*

(29) *Nancy Reagan. She further defended the new china by saying it had been purchased by the Knapp Foundation and donated to the White House. And, she added, the White House was ready for new china because the last time a new set had been purchased was during the Truman Administration.*

(30) *President William McKinley. Anarchist Leon F. Czolgosz shot the pres-*

ident on the afternoon of September 6, 1901. The president died about one week later.

㉛ *(b) Adlai Stevenson.*

㉜ *Phyllis Schlafly. Arch rival of the National Organization for Women, she lobbied hard against passage of the Equal Rights Amendment.*

㉝ *Thomas Jefferson. He demonstrated his opposition to slavery by signing legislation in 1807 that outlawed the importation of slaves.*

㉞ *Lyndon B. Johnson.*

㉟ *John Sirica. After being involved in the five year Watergate trial from start to finish, he concluded in* To Set The Record Straight *that had he not resigned first, Nixon would have been convicted during the senate impeachment trial, because "no self-respecting politician could ignore the hard evidence."*

㊱ *Jimmy Carter.*

㊲ *George Burns. This quip was uncharacteristic of Burns whose humor in radio, television and film was seldom of a political nature. He was best known for his part in the comedy team of Burns and Allen with his wife, Gracie Allen.*

⊗ *Thomas Paine. These remarks came from* The American Crisis, *a series of pamphlets written in 1776 that were read to George Washington's troops to build up their confidence. Paine might be better known for another pamphlet,* Common Sense.

㊴ *Martin Luther King. The charismatic orator was, of course well-known for his "I have a dream" speech.*

㊵ *(a) President John F. Kennedy, (b) "I am a Berliner," and (c) while on a ten-day tour of Europe in June 1963, he spoke to a crowd of West Berliners and said, "All free men, wherever they may live, are citizens of Berlin. And, therefore, as a free man, I take pride in the words, 'Ich bin ein Berliner.' "*

㊶ *Franklin D. Roosevelt. This was the first time, during the 1932 Democratic nominating convention in Chicago, that he used the term "new deal," lifting it from the pages of Mark Twain's* A Connecticut Yankee in King Arthur's Court. *The news media liked the phrase, and it became the name for his reform package.*

㊷ *Franklin D. Roosevelt. He used that phrase in his first inaugural speech speaking to the fearful nation in the midst of the Great Depression in March, 1933.*

④③ *"The buck stops here."*
He was borrowing from the poker expression "passing
the buck." Not afraid of the responsibilities of the
presidency, Truman is also quoted as saying, "If you
can't stand the heat, get out of the kitchen."

④④ *Richard Nixon. He*
made these comments while addressing a convention
of Associated Press editors in November 1973 at Dis-

neyworld in Florida in the midst of the Watergate investigation. Four months later he was named as a coconspirator by a federal grand jury.

④⑤ *Benjamin Franklin. He said this when he signed the Declaration of Independence on July 4, 1776.*

④⑥ *President Jimmy Carter. On April 19, 1977, the president went on national television to convince skeptical Americans that the country was in the midst of an energy crisis. He said lifestyle changes would have to be made in order to win the energy "war."*

④⑦ *Lyndon B. Johnson, in his reflections on the presidency in* The Vantage Point: Perspectives of the Presidency, *published in 1971.*

④⑧ *General Douglas Mac-Arthur. He was making reference to an old ballad and continued, "and like the old soldier in that ballad, I now close my military career and just fade away, an old soldier who tried to do his duty as God gave him the sight to see that duty."*

④⑨ *Harry Truman.*

⑤⓪ *Herbert Hoover. He made this speech in 1928, a few months before the stock market crash and the depression that followed.*

International
Politics

Although this book is primarily about American politics, we can't forget about the individuals and institutions around the world that influence the policies and diplomacy of the United States.

Let's see how much you know about some of the better-known world leaders, the things they've said and their struggles to gain and hold on to power.

❶ Archbishop Makarios was president of this small eastern Mediterranean island that became a republic in 1960, free of British rule. Name the island.

❷ Soviet leader Mikhail Gorbachev introduced a policy of "openness" in 1986. What did he call it?

3 President Carter was host to the first Chinese Communist leader to visit the United States. Name the leader.

4 Eleven Israeli athletes were gunned down by Arab guerillas during the 1972 Olympics. (a) Where were the Olympics held that year, and (b) what terrorist group was responsible for the brutal attack on the Olympic village?

5 In 1988 Benazir Bhutto became the first woman to lead a Muslim nation. She was the prime minister of what country?

6 Who was the Japanese emperor who left his nation speechless by announcing that imperial divinity, the theory that the emperor was a descendant of the sun god, was a fallacy?

7 Let's see how much you know about the Arab-Israeli wars. Here's a two-parter: (a) Egypt suffered an abysmal defeat at the hands of Israel in 1967. What was the name of the short war? (b) In 1973 Israel was attacked by Egypt, Syria, and Iraq on its most holy day of the year. Name the war.

8 Name the four children of Queen Elizabeth II and Philip Mountbatten, Duke of Edinburgh. Which one is first in the line of succession for the throne?

9 In 1979 Muhammad Reza Shah Pahlavi was ousted as leader of this Middle Eastern country after having been in power for thirty-seven years. For this three-parter: (a) name the country, (b) give the name by which Pahlevi is better known, and (c) name the person who supplanted him.

10 Name the U.S. ship seized along with its thirty-nine-member crew by Cambodian gunboats in 1975.

11 What is another name for the 1991 war in the Persian Gulf?

12 The name of the battle that proved to be Napoleon Bonaparte's downfall has become a term used to describe a major career-ending defeat. Name the battle.

13 Here's a two-parter. After the Communists took control of South Vietnam and united it with the North, creating the Socialist Republic of Vietnam, (a) what city became the capital, and (b) what was the name of Saigon changed to?

14 Name the Latin American revolutionary leader who served as Fidel Castro's right hand man during the Cuban revolution in 1959, and whose name became synonymous with left-wing radicalism.

⓯ This man was president-for-life of a southeastern European country, ruling for thirty-five years with the help of a strong secret police force. Name the man and the country.

⓰ Egypt's president throughout the 1970s was co-recipient of the 1978 Nobel Peace Prize. For this two-parter: (a) name the president, and (b) name his successor.

⓱ After twenty-four years of British control, Sri Lanka became an island republic in 1972. Was its former name (a) Burma, (b) Thailand, or (c) Ceylon?

⓲ Name the Soviet leader who was known for using his shoe as a gavel at the United Nations and for the historic words "we will bury you."

⓳ What is the British counterpart to the U.S. Constitution?

⓴ Like most countries, India has many political factions, some of them an outcropping of different religious sects. The 1984 assassination of the prime minister of India was motivated by religious causes. Who was the prime minister and who were the assassins?

㉑ Which country was the first to recognize the newly created state of

Israel in 1948? For extra points, who was Israel's first president?

22 Robert Mugabe was instrumental in gaining independence for this African country, becoming its first prime minister in 1980. By what name do we know this country today, and what is its former name?

23 In 1980 a Soviet nuclear physicist was exiled from his home for his outspoken opposition to the USSR's presence in Afghanistan and to human rights violations in the USSR. Who is he?

24 In 1949 the Communists deposed Chiang Kai-shek and created the People's Republic of China. Who became the Republic's new chairman?

25 Here's a follow-up question. Driven from the Chinese mainland, Chiang Kai-shek created a new government on an island in the Pacific, becoming the president of Nationalist China. Name the island.

26 Name the first Premier of the Congo who was ousted one year after taking office, and whose death raised questions of foul play. Was it (a) Joseph Mobutu, (b) Patrice Lumumba, or (c) Joseph Kasavubu?

27 Give the names of the allied nations and of their leaders during World War II.

28 Who was the leader of the Polish labor union Solidarity, arrested in December of 1981 for his demonstrations against the Polish government? For extra credit, what elected position does he now hold?

29 What organization was created in 1949 to safeguard the North Atlantic community of nations against the Soviet powers. For extra credit, name as many of the sixteen members as you can.

30 This northwest African country gained its independence from France in 1962, led by Ben Bella, who became the nation's first president. Was it (a) Algeria, (b) Niger, or (c) Libya?

31 Hunger strikes, bombings, and other terrorist attacks have characterized the tactics used by this organization, intent upon eliminating British rule in Northern Ireland and unifying the entire country. Name the organization.

32 He became King of Spain in 1975, handpicked by his predecessor, a dictator who had ruled the country for thirty-six years. Can you name (a) the king, and (b) the former ruler?

33 This rebellion took place in China, from 1898 to 1900, resulting in members of an anti-foreign organization murdering western missionaries and Chinese Christians. What was it called?

34 François Mitterand, Valéry Giscard d'Estaing, Charles De Gaulle, and Georges Pompidou have all served as president of France. See if you can place them in the order in which they served.

35 Here's a follow-up question. Which of the four French presidents mentioned above was the first socialist president of the Fifth Republic?

36 Israeli commandos rescued ninety-one hostages at an airport in this south Ugandan town in 1976. Was it (a) Kampala, (b) Entebbe, or (c) Nairobi?

37 Here's another follow-up question. The president of Uganda, who allegedly supported the hijackers and provided them with weapons, ruled with terroristic tactics himself from 1971 to 1979. Name him.

38 For more than nine years, civil war between the Sandinista government and the Contras has raged in this country. What is the country?

39 Name the Emperor of Ethiopia who was in power for fifty-eight years until he was ousted in 1974 by a military coup.

40 Sentiment for the entry of the United States into World War I was aroused when a German submarine sank a British liner carrying more than 125 Americans. Name the ship.

41 François Duvalier, a self-proclaimed "president-for-life," was the dictator of Haiti for fourteen years. By what name was he best known?

42 France, Italy, Chile, Guinea, and Indonesia all have the same form of government. What is it?

43 In May 1987 an Iraqi fighter fired on an American frigate in the Persian Gulf, killing thirty-seven Americans. Name the vessel.

44 Early in 1968 North Vietnam launched a new offensive attack against the United States and South Vietnamese forces. The attack, spanned over one hundred cities, fueled anti-war demonstrations in the United States. What was that strategy called?

45 Let's see how well you know the leaders of various countries. Match their name on the left with the nations they govern.

Leader	Country
1. Frederik De Klerk	(a) Greece
2. Prince Norodom Sihanouk	(b) Syria
3. Brian Mulroney	(c) Indonesia
4. Lieutenant General Hafez al-Assad	(d) South Africa
5. Helmut Kohl	(e) Monaco
6. Carl XVI Gustaf	(f) Canada
7. Andreas Papandreou	(g) West Germany
8. Suharto	(h) Cambodia
9. Prince Ranier III	(i) Philippines
10. Corazon Aquino	(j) Sweden

46 Name the court that hears international disputes between members of the United Nations.

47 This commando leader became the head of the Palestine Liberation Organization in 1969. Name him.

48 In 1964 the Soviet Communist party removed Nikita Kruschev as its First Secretary and as Soviet Premier. The two positions were then filled by two separate men. Who were they?

49 In 1914 the assassination of a world leader was the immediate cause of World War I. Name the victim and his assassin.

50 Russian revolutionary Vladimir Ilyich Ulyanov took on a pen name in 1901. What was it?

51 After the death of the Soviet leader mentioned in the preceding question, Joseph Stalin entered into a power struggle with another Russian revolutionary. Who was he and who was the victor?

52 Who was Hitler's Enlightenment and Propaganda Minister who killed his wife and six children before committing suicide as Germany's defeat to the Allies became inevitable?

53 African politico Sésé Séko Mobutu changed the name of the Congo while he served as its president. What is its present name?

54 Who was the leader of Libya when the United States attacked that country on April 16, 1986?

55 He was Israel's first prime minister and the man who played the most influential role for that country in its early years. Name him.

56 To some, political power plays second fiddle to love. For this two-parter: (a) name the king who gave up his throne in 1936, and (b) name the woman for whom he gave it up.

57 A Swedish diplomat served as Secretary-General of the United Nations in the 1950s, focusing his involvement in the Congo. He died when his plane crashed over Northern Rhodesia. Who was he?

58 Follow-up question: Who succeeded the man in the previous question as Secretary-General of the United Nations, helping to resolve the Cuban missile crisis and the 1967 war between Israel and the Arabs?

59 The corrupt Filipino regime of President Ferdinand Marcos was ousted in February of 1986. Who took power?

60 Ferdinand Marcos's wife, Imelda, had a shoe fetish, amassing quite a collection of footwear. How many pairs did she leave behind when they fled to Hawaii?

61 A Panamanian leader faced U.S. indictments in 1988. For this two-parter: (a) who was the leader, and (b) what were the charges?

62 This British colony will revert to Chinese sovereignty in 1997. Name it.

63 What twentieth-century Soviet leader remarked, "Politicians are the same all over. They promise to build a bridge even when there is no river." Was it: (a) Karl Marx, (b) Joseph Stalin, or (c) Nikita Khrushchev?

64 What twentieth-century British prime minister said: "Politics are almost as exciting as war, and quite as dangerous. In war, you can only be killed once, but in politics many times."

65 What Chinese Communist leader said that "political power grows out of the barrel of a gun"?

66 What European leader knew this only too well: "The great masses of the people . . . will more easily fall victim to a great lie than a small one"?

67 What president of a European country during the 1960s remarked, "How can you govern a country with two hundred and forty-six varieties of cheeses?" Was it: (a) Charles De Gaulle, (b) Margaret Thatcher, or (c) Willy Brandt?

68 Margaret Thatcher became the first woman prime minister of Great Britain in 1979. Who was her predecessor, and who replaced her in 1990?

69 Who was the first prime minister of the Republic of India after it broke away in 1947 from what became Pakistan?

70 Here's a two-parter: (a) who was the South African political activist sentenced to life imprisonment in 1964 for his antiapartheid activities but released in 1990, and (b) who was the prime minister who released him?

71 Name the black South African bishop who has crusaded against apartheid through nonviolence.

72 What are the two major political parties in Great Britain?

73 Britain's former secretary of war brought disgrace to himself and Prime Minister Harold Macmillan in 1963 when he was accused of having an affair with a prostitute. Name (a) the politician, and (b) the woman implicated in the affair.

74 Name the Indian political and religious leader whose belief in nonviolence and passive resistance became the model for Martin Luther King, Jr. and other activists.

Answers

① *Cyprus. The Orthodox Eastern archbishop was elected president three times and survived four assassination attempts.*

② *Glasnost.*

③ *Deputy Premier Deng Xiaoping. He visited the United States in 1979.*

④ *(a) Munich, Germany. (b) Black September. The terrorists took the athletes hostage, demanding that Palestinian prisoners be released from Israeli prisons.*

⑤ *Pakistan. She is the daughter of Ali Bhutto, Pakistan's president throughout the 1970s, who was ousted in 1977 and later hanged for his involvement in a politically instigated murder.*

⑥ *Emperor Hirohito. He made his historic proclamation in 1946, the same year he lost most of his power through the adoption of the country's new constitution.*

⑦ *(a) The Six-Day War. It resulted in the reuniting of Jerusalem. (b) The Yom Kippur War. The Israelis were able to push back the aggressors, but not without losing more than 1,800 soldiers.*

⑧ *Charles, Anne, Andrew, and Edward. Prince Charles is first in line for the throne.*

⑨ *(a) Iran, (b) the Shah of Iran, and (c) the Ayatollah Khomeini.*

⑩ *The* Mayaguez. *The United States was able to free the vessel and crew, but the successful rescue ended in forty-one American deaths.*

⑪ *Operation Desert Storm.*

⑫ *Waterloo. He was soundly defeated at this last battle of the Napoleonic Wars in June of 1815. British and Prussian forces trounced Napoleon's troops, causing the French leader to abdicate.*

⑬ *(a) The capital city of the Socialist Republic of Vietnam became Hanoi, and (b) Saigon became Ho Chi Minh City.*

⑭ *"Che" Ernesto Guevara. He later served as Castro's minister of industry from 1961 until 1965, when he left Cuba. He led a revolution in Bolivia in 1966, but was executed there the following year.*

⑮ *Josip Tito of Yugoslavia. He made an historic split with Joseph Stalin in 1948, liberating the country from Soviet control.*

⑯ *Anwar al-Sadat, who was a co-recipient of the 1978 Nobel Peace Prize. He was assassinated in 1981 by fanatic Moslems serving in the military, possibly angered by Egypt's peace treaty with Israel. Muhammad Mubarak, Sadat's vice president, was his successor.*

⑰ *(c) Ceylon. The Democratic Socialist Republic of Sri Lanka is located southeast of India in the Indian Ocean.*

⑱ *Nikita Khruschev. Khruschev was removed from office in 1964, partly because of his inability to foster better relations with China. This once powerful man lived an obscure existence from 1969 until his death seven years later.*

⑲ *The Magna Carta, the "great charter" of English liberties. It was signed by King John at Runnymede on June 15, 1215. The English barons forced King John to sign the document.*

⑳ *Indira Gandhi. She took office in 1966, served eleven years before her ouster, and made a comeback in 1980. Her two assassins were members of the Sikh faith, seeking retaliation for the government's attack on their temple.*

㉑ *The United States was the first country to recognize the new state of Israel in 1948, followed by the Soviet Union. Dr. Chaim Weizmann was its first president.*

㉒ *The country, Zimbabwe, formerly Rhodesia, was created in 1980. Mugabe led Rhodesia's largest guerilla force in its independence from Great Britain.*

㉓ *Andrei Sakharov. In 1975 he became the first citizen of the USSR to receive the Nobel Peace Prize. He and his wife Yelena Bonner came out of their six-year exile when he was pardoned by Mikhail Gorbachev in 1986.*

㉔ *Mao Tse-Tung. He and President Nixon met in 1972, improving relations between the United States and China.*

㉕ *Taiwan.*

㉖ *(b) Patrice Lumumba. His death was explained away by saying he was killed during a prison escape attempt, but lack of cooperation in the investigation of his death caused suspicion of a politically motivated murder.*

㉗ *United States President Franklin D. Roosevelt, Great Britain's Winston Churchill, and Soviet Premier Joseph Stalin were known as the "Big Three."*

㉘ *Lech Walesa. He was released eleven months later, received the Nobel Peace Prize in 1983, and was elected president of Poland in 1990.*

㉙ *Nato (The North Atlan-*

tic Treaty Organization). Headquartered in Brussels, its members include Belgium, Canada, Denmark, France, Great Britain, Greece, Iceland, Italy, Luxembourg, the Netherlands, Norway, Portugal, Spain, Turkey, the United States, and West Germany.

㉚ *(a) Algeria. Ben Bella was ousted in 1965 by the leader of the military government, Colonel Houari Boumedienne.*

㉛ *The Irish Republican Army (IRA).*

㉜ *(a) King Juan Carlos. (b) Francisco Franco. He declared Spain a monarchy in 1947 and himself its "regent." Six years before his death in 1975 he appointed Prince Juan Carlos, grandson of the former King Alfonso VIII, as the king in waiting.*

㉝ *The Boxer Rebellion. The goal of the secret Chinese organization, the Boxers, was to oust all foreigners from the country. The royal court secretly supported the terrorist activities of the group. It required military intervention by the United States, Europe, Russia, and Japan to quash the uprising, eventually ending in the signing of a treaty on September 7, 1901.*

㉞ *De Gaulle was the first president, in office from 1959 to 1969. (He was fol-*

lowed by Pompidou (1969–1974), Giscard d'Estaing (1974–1981) and Mitterrand, 1981 to the present.

㉟ *François Mitterrand.*

㊱ *(b) Entebbe. While holding the hostages, primarily Israelis and other Jews, on an airplane, the pro-Palestinian terrorists demanded that fifty-three prisoners be released from Israeli and European prisons.*

㊲ *Idi Amin. His eight years of tyrannical power brought the deterioration of Uganda. He executed about 300,000 Ugandans and expelled an estimated 50,000 Asians.*

㊳ *Nicaragua. The United States has provided the right wing Contras with money and supplies.*

㊴ *Haile Selassie. The ouster ended the monarchy system that had existed in Ethiopia since the tenth century B.C. The military leaders established a socialist state in 1975.*

㊵ *The* Lusitania. *Germany responded to President Woodrow Wilson's indignation by saying that Americans had been warned of the possibility of such attacks.*

㊶ *"Papa Doc." His nickname came from the fact that he was a doctor. A merciless dictator, his years in power were a "reign of terror." His son, Jean-Claude Duvalier, "Baby*

Doc," became his successor when Papa Doc died in 1971.

④② *A republic. A republic is a sovereignty governed by elected administrators and legislators.*

④③ *The U.S.S. Stark. The ship was in the gulf to protect the oil shipping interests of the United States during the Iran-Iraq War. Iraq apologized for what it claimed was an accident.*

④④ *The Tet offensive. Although it was considered a failure for the North Vietnamese, the Tet offensive became a strong rallying point for anti-war demonstrations in the United States.*

④⑤ *1(d), 2(h), 3(f), 4(b), 5(g), 6(j), 7(a), 8(c), 9(e), 10(i)*

④⑥ *The International Court of Justice. Fifteen judges, selected by the United Nations General Assembly and Security Council sit on the court. Its decisions cannot be appealed.*

④⑦ *Yasar Arafat.*

④⑧ *First Secretary—Leonid Brezhnev, Premier—Aleksei Kosygin.*

④⑨ *Austria-Hungary's Archduke Francis Ferdinand was killed by a Serbian nationalist, Gavrilo Princip.*

㊿ *Vladimir Ilyich Lenin. He was a Russian revolutionary leader, credited with founding the USSR as well as Bolshevism. "Lenin" was only one of about seventy-five pseudonyms that he used.*

51 *Leon Trotsky. He was an advocate of a world revolution, while Stalin's main concern was socialism in the Soviet Union. Stalin won in the power struggle, and Trotsky was eventually ousted from the country in 1929. In his writings, Trotsky continued to speak out against Stalin. Trotsky was murdered eleven years later in Mexico City.*

52 *Joseph Goebbels. He served as Hitler's propaganda minister in 1933.*

53 *Zaire. In 1966 Mobutu and his followers ousted Joseph Kasavubu. Mobutu became prime minister of the Belgian Congo. The next year he created a new form of government, assuming the presidency, and changing its name to Zaire in 1971.*

54 *Colonel Muammar al-Qaddafi. President Reagan had ordered the Libyan attack in retaliation for the April 4, 1986 devastation by the Libyans of a West Berlin discotheque filled with American servicemen.*

⑤⑤ *David Ben-Gurion. He was Israel's prime minister from 1948 to 1953 and again from 1955 to 1963. He formed the Rafi Party after the Labour Party expelled him in 1965.*

⑤⑥ *(a) King Edward VIII succeeded to the throne of England on January 20, 1936, at his father's death, but abdicated on December 11, 1936, (b) so that he could marry Wallis Warfield Simpson, an American divorcee. Edward, thereafter known as the Duke of Windsor, abdicated in favor of his brother, who became George VI, Queen Elizabeth II's father.*

⑤⑦ *Dag Hammarskjöld. His diplomatic successes as an official with the United Nations earned him a Nobel Peace Prize, awarded posthumously in 1961.*

⑤⑧ *U Thant. Formerly a Burmese diplomat, he served as Secretary-General of the United Nations from 1962 to 1972.*

⑤⑨ *Corazon Aquino. Marcos won the 1986 election fraudulently, but an insurrection by Filipinos and the army put Aquino in power. A few weeks later the United States granted "full diplomatic recognition" to her government. Marcos fled to Hawaii after the ouster and died there in October of 1989 of a heart attack.*

60 *1060 pairs of shoes. It was reported that she had two pairs of battery-operated shoes that lit up. Her love of clothing evidently did not end with shoes: she left behind over 500 floor-length gowns, 427 dresses, and 888 purses.*

61 *Drug smuggling. Noriega was also charged with using Panamanian banks to launder drug money.*

62 *Hong Kong. It was occupied by Great Britain during the Opium War from 1839 to 1842, was taken over by Japan during World War II, and reclaimed by England in 1945. In 1997 it will become the Hong Kong Special Administrative Region of China.*

63 *(a) Nikita Khrushchev.*

64 *Winston Churchill. Having been both a celebrated statesman and soldier, he may be one of the most qualified men to compare both roles.*

65 *(a) Mao Tse-Tung. He himself achieved political power "out of the barrel of a gun" creating the People's Republic of China through revolution and serving as its first chairman, beginning in 1949.*

66 *Adolph Hitler. This quote came from* Mein Kampf *(My Struggle). Written while Hitler was in prison for nine months in 1923, this book became the bible of Nazism.*

⑥⑦ *(a) Charles De Gaulle. He became president of France in 1959 and held that office until 1969.*

⑥⑧ *James Callaghan was Thatcher's predecessor. She was succeeded by John Major.*

⑥⑨ *Jawaharlal Nehru. He was the first prime minister of the Republic of India after it broke away from what became Pakistan in 1947. The Nehru jacket was all the rage with United States college students during the late 1960s and early 1970s.*

⑦⓪ *(a) Nelson Mandela. He became the anti-apartheid symbol to the world through his imprisonment. (b) Frederik W. De Klerk. After replacing Pieter Botha as prime minister in September 1989, he released Mandela from prison in February 1990.*

⑦① *Bishop Desmond Tutu. A recipient of the 1984 Nobel Peace Prize, Tutu has attempted to eliminate apartheid in South Africa through nonviolent methods, particularly economic sanctions.*

⑦② *The Labour and Conservative parties are Great Britain's major political parties.*

⑦③ *(a) John Dennis Profumo and (b) Christine Keeler. Profumo resigned his position on June 5, 1963. Prime Minister Macmillan's reputation was tarnished as well. He was accused of not acting more promptly to investigate the incident.*

(74) *Mohandas (Mahatma) Gandhi. He brought about India's independence through a nonviolent revolution. He conducted life-threatening fasts to end the caste system in India and the violence between Hindus and Muslims.*